MY GREATEST FOOTBALL TEAM EVER

Written by
TOM FORDYCE
Illustrations by
KIERAN CARROLL

wren
& rook

For Arthur and Jonty,
the source of so many
sporting questions.
As well as my favourite
two people in the world
to watch football with.

CONTENTS

CONTENTS

BUILD YOUR DREAM TEAM

Imagine being the manager of Liverpool, or **Barcelona, or England, or Manchester City.** The players you'd get to work with, the quality of the football, the absolutely unbelievable levels of skill you'd be witnessing every day. The free stuff, the challenges, the power and the glory.

That's decent. It's a job to dream of. Now imagine not simply having the best players at that club, but from **anywhere in the world**. And not just now, but from any point since the dinosaurs died off and prehistoric man started booting rocks about.

The finest players **that have ever lived**, in every single position, available for you to choose. And coach. And motivate. And **beat everyone else** out of sight with.

Deep breaths. This is **big**. The greatest football team ever. **Run by you.** More breaths, because actually this gets **bigger**. This team will need a name. You'll need a big-name assistant to help out with the coaching. A kit will have to be designed, and a club badge, and a mascot. What formation will it use? Who will sponsor the shirts, and what will the stadium look like?

ALL OF IT IS DOWN TO YOU.

Over the following pages you'll find facts, stats and detailed descriptions of eight possible players for each position. Do your scouting, chew it over with those you trust, check these superstars' highlights out online.

When you're ready – when you've considered all the options, had all the arguments, anguished about the brutally difficult decisions – make your **big selection**. One player chosen above all others in each position, inked in as part of an 11-strong team superior to anything the world has ever seen before.

We have players from **down the ages**, from 60 years ago, from 20 years ago. We have the finest women footballers of all time. You might think the speed and physical demands of the modern game would be too much for a few players who shone under different conditions. But that would be to deny some of the **most skilful players in history** their rightful place. If a footballer has proved their greatness in their own era or at the highest level available to them, they're in. It's all about the very best.

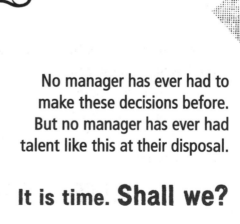

No manager has ever had to make these decisions before. But no manager has ever had talent like this at their disposal.

It is time. Shall we?

YOU, THE MANAGER

First things first. Before you even start to consider **selecting** your team, you need to decide **what sort of boss** you're going to be. **Cool** like Pep? Noisy and **fun** like Klopp? A bit like a **nice teacher**, if you're a fan of Gareth Southgate?

Circle the words and phrases that make you the boss to lead your team to victory. There's no right or wrong. Only you.

 **TRACKSUIT** **OR** *suit/tie/ waistcoat*

 OR *cool shirt and jumper*

 **DOES FUNNY INTERVIEWS** **OR** **TREATS FOOTBALL AS SERIOUS BUSINESS**

 **STAYS ON BENCH** **OR** **JUMPS AROUND LOTS**

ANGRY **OR** calm

LEARNS THE LOCAL LANGUAGE **OR** JUST SHOUTS A LOT

hugs players **OR** stays aloof

joins in training **OR** SITS ON THE SIDELINES AND WATCHES

buys **pizza** for players when they **win** **OR** bans chips from canteen

calls players by surnames **OR** **CALLS PLAYERS BY NICKNAMES**

←maverick→ **OR** traditional

NAME THAT TEAM

Next you're going to need a team name. This could be straightforward. **Where your team is based + United.** Easy ...

Easy, but hardly **original!** There were **14 Citys**, **13 Uniteds** and **12 Towns** in the top four leagues of English football in the 2019-20 season.

So, feel free to be creative here – your street, your house or flat number. And while location is a good start, there are so many other options to pair it with. **Rovers. Wanderers. Albion.** The one-offs like Villa or Argyle.

Maybe work in a notable local feature, as in **Nottingham Forest**, River Plate or Warwick Motorway Services. Or the day of the week when you want to play matches, like Sheffield Wednesday or **Knutsford Tuesday Evenings**.

A simple **Something FC** (as in 'Football Club') works. Be funky and switch it around, European-style: 'FC Something' always adds glamour and a certain style. Or borrow from the best and be **Real Somewhere**.

* *

```
             SCOUTING REPORT:
             ----------------
'Real' here comes from the Spanish word for
ROYAL, meaning a KING OR QUEEN supports you,
rather than the opposite of fake. Is your style
of football going to be SO SWEET that you get
the royal seal of approval?
```

* *

Teams from **exotic places** love to feature a fierce creature – the Adelaide Cobras, the California Jaguars. Just make sure you choose one with bite. The **Harlow Hedgehogs** would scare no-one …

You could even name them after **you**. Yes, it's big-headed. But who's to say that **Rapid Raymond** doesn't have a certain ring to it?

So, what's it going to be?
Once you've decided, engrave it into the plaque below.

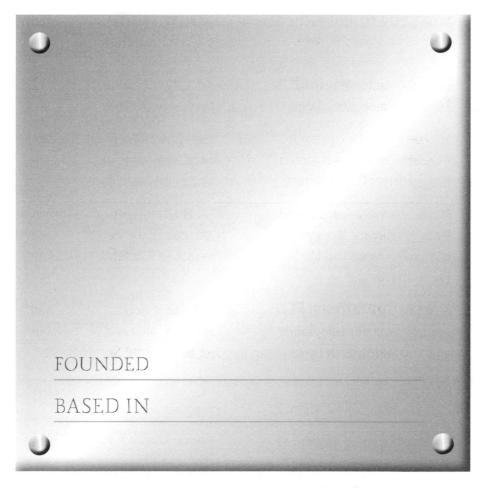

FOUNDED

BASED IN

So, you've got your management style. You've got your team name. Now it's time for the big stuff: picking the players who are going to make up the greatest team in history.

Let's start in style with the number ones... Strikers get the glamour. Wingers get the flashy boots. Goalkeepers? 'Keepers keep it real. You can trust a great goalkeeper. Brave. Calm, mainly. Slightly mad, in a good way.

A team without a great goalie is like a sports car without wheels: it might look cool, but it's going nowhere. A striker makes a mistake, and nothing happens to the score. A goalie makes one slip and it's a goal for the other side. Ouch. Yet they can be the hero. Diving full-length to fingertip away a shot heading top bins. Sticking out a foot to deny a striker who's already celebrating. Pick the right goalie, and you too might end up number one.

And so this is a selection that needs careful thought. You need someone who can make saves so impossible that you can't quite believe what's just happened. You need someone who can rule their area, go the right way on penalties and throw themselves at the feet of a charging striker just about to shoot. They have to be strong, agile as an Olympic gymnast and capable of organising their defence. A loud voice is more important than big hands. They need co-ordination, concentration and self-belief.

Goalkeepers are different. You can't manage them like other players. You'll need to work out what makes them tick. This is not an easy choice. But you're no ordinary manager. Let's do this.

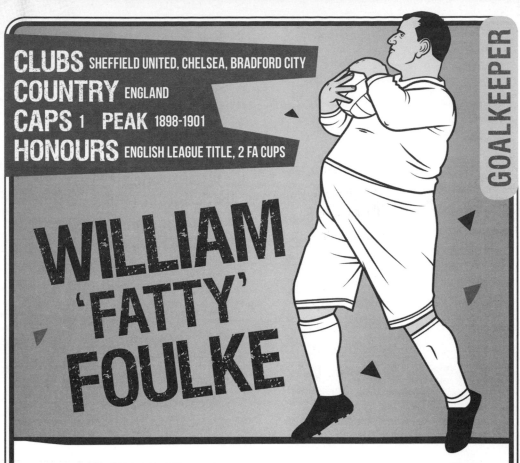

CLUBS SHEFFIELD UNITED, CHELSEA, BRADFORD CITY
COUNTRY ENGLAND
CAPS 1 **PEAK** 1898-1901
HONOURS ENGLISH LEAGUE TITLE, 2 FA CUPS

WILLIAM 'FATTY' FOULKE

There is **so much** to like about Fatty Foulke. Not least that he was happy to be called **Fatty**. When you're **twice as big** as any other player on your team, you're **twice as hard to beat.**

Fatty played in the era **before goalie gloves**, when shorts came halfway to your chin and strikers were allowed to **shoulder-barge** you. And he was a **genius** despite all that. Incredibly **nimble** for a man so big. Inventor of the **long kicked clearance**, when most 'keepers went short and feeble. Imagine being clean through on goal, looking up and seeing a giant charging towards you. **Exactly.**

But he's going to take some **looking after**. On one occasion he got **so** angry with a referee that he chased him into a cupboard. **Naked.** If opposition strikers annoyed him he **picked them up** and threw them into the goal.

Best of all: he once **sneaked down early** at the team hotel and ate **all** of his team-mates' breakfasts. Ten of them, plus his own. **Respect.**

SHOT STOPPING	COMMAND OF BOX	DISTRIBUTION	YOUR RATING
7/10	9/10	7/10	/10

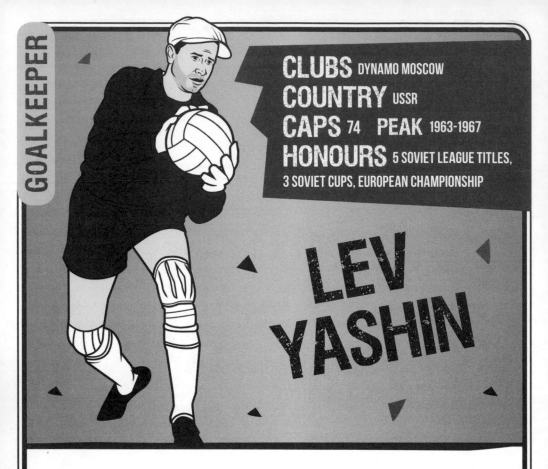

CLUBS DYNAMO MOSCOW
COUNTRY USSR
CAPS 74   **PEAK** 1963-1967
HONOURS 5 SOVIET LEAGUE TITLES, 3 SOVIET CUPS, EUROPEAN CHAMPIONSHIP

LEV YASHIN

What a player. What a **look:** black jersey, black shorts, baggy cap. What a **record: more penalties saved** than any other 'keeper in history.

They called him the **Black Spider,** because **nothing** could get past those arms and legs of his, except when they called him the **Black Panther,** because he could **leap** so far and so fast.

Yashin **invented** modern goalkeeping: playing it out short to his full-backs, **coming out of his box** to boot the ball clear, **punching** crosses like Tyson Fury.

He **shouted** at his defence and it worked; he was an **organiser** so good it was like having an extra coach on the pitch. But he took losses hard, and if he made a mistake he could **brood** on it for days.

You're going to have to work on his moods. He'll tell you **exactly** what he thinks, which might be uncomfortable. **But he's worth it.**

| SHOT STOPPING | **9/10** | COMMAND OF BOX | **10/10** | DISTRIBUTION | **8/10** | YOUR RATING | **/10** |

CLUBS MANCHESTER CITY
COUNTRY GERMANY
CAPS 0 **PEAK** 1950-1956
HONOURS FA CUP

BERT TRAUTMANN

Bert was pure bravery. An **innovator** too – throwing the ball out to keep possession for his team, the first footballer in England to wear **adidas boots**. But **guts** like no other. Don't worry about the lack of international caps either. Back then, West Germany **wouldn't pick players** who played their club football overseas, and Bert chose to stay in England, where he'd been a **prisoner of war**, after the Second World War.

As a **soldier** Trautmann saw some **horrific** battles. He was the **only man** of the original 90 in his regiment to make it through alive. But what he did afterwards was more remarkable.

The 1956 FA Cup final, Trautmann already City's outstanding player. City 3–1 up when the 'keeper **threw himself** at the feet of an onrushing striker. **Bang. Knocked out.** Then he got back to his feet and **carried on playing**. Only afterwards did he discover he had also **broken his neck,** an injury that could have **killed** him! Playing with five dislocated vertebrae? He's like the anti-Neymar. There's courage, and then there's **Bert.**

SHOT STOPPING	7/10	COMMAND OF BOX	7/10	DISTRIBUTION	8/10	YOUR RATING	/10

CLUBS CHESTERFIELD, LEICESTER CITY, STOKE CITY, FORT LAUDERDALE

COUNTRY ENGLAND
CAPS 73

PEAK 1966-1970
HONOURS WORLD CUP, 2 LEAGUE CUPS

GORDON BANKS

It might seem harsh on Peter Shilton to pick Banks ahead of him. Shilts took Banks' place for both club and country. He played **more times** for England.

But Banks was **Shilton's hero,** and he is going to give you so much. The hard work of a man whose first job was **lugging sacks of coal**. The quiet dedication of someone whose first contract paid him just **£3 per week**. The springiness and skills of an **acrobat**. Banks is the **only goalkeeper** to win the World Cup for England. It wasn't even his greatest moment.

1970 World Cup, England v Brazil. A bullet of a downward header from Pelé, Banks **stranded** at his near post, Pelé and half the crowd already shouting, **'GOAL!'** Then a **blur** of movement. Banks **diving** back and across, the ball bouncing up and in – until somehow Banks' right hand was there, flicking the ball **up and over** the crossbar.

Many say it was the **single greatest save** ever seen. And if he could save that, he could save **anything**.

SHOT STOPPING	COMMAND OF BOX	DISTRIBUTION	YOUR RATING
10/10	7/10	7/10	/10

CLUBS PARMA, JUVENTUS, PARIS SAINT-GERMAIN
COUNTRY ITALY
CAPS 176   **PEAK** 2002-2006
HONOURS 9 ITALIAN LEAGUE TITLES, WORLD CUP, UEFA CUP, 5 ITALIAN CUPS, FRENCH LEAGUE TITLE

GIANLUIGI BUFFON

Pick Buffon and you're getting a man who made **diving around in the mud** look like the **greatest thing ever invented.**

His record is **sensational:** a debut for Italy as a **teenager**, conceding **only two goals** (one a penalty, the other an own-goal) all tournament as Italy won the 2006 World Cup; the **most clean sheets** in Italian League history, the most for Italy. **Quality.**

He could be **stroppy** and so he might be a handful for you on the pitch. And as an Italian, he might kiss you when you win. There are definitely better 'keepers on **crosses** too.

But **whoah**, was he **cool.** Always a short-sleeved shirt, because he liked the **feel** of the ball on his arms. Almost always **stylish hair**; sometimes a pink jersey, sometimes gold.

Passion, drama, crazy ability. Buffon stopped shots other 'keepers could only **watch** fly past.

SHOT STOPPING	10/10	COMMAND OF BOX	7/10	DISTRIBUTION	7/10	YOUR RATING	/10

CLUBS PHILADELPHIA CHARGE, GOTHENBURG, LYON, SAINT LOUIS ATHLETICA, ATLANTA BEAT, MAGICJACK, SEATTLE SOUNDERS, SEATTLE REIGN

COUNTRY USA
CAPS 202 **PEAK** 2008-2012
HONOURS
WORLD CUP, 2 OLYMPIC GOLDS

HOPE SOLO

Hope has done things no other goalkeeper could do. Fifty-five games of international football without conceding a goal. More than **200 appearances** for the US and **only 11 defeats**. Twice voted the **best goalkeeper** at a World Cup.

But Hope might also bring you **despair**. She was quite happy to **publicly criticise** her coach and fellow players and she was **twice** suspended by the US team for bad behaviour.

Yet she could make **low saves** that defied belief. Her **timing** off her line was perfection. She was **decisive** and made the penalty box her own.

Still, it's those low saves that really **blow your mind.** Germany's Nadine Angerer could do almost anything. She couldn't go **Solo** like Hope.

SHOT STOPPING	10/10	COMMAND OF BOX	8/10	DISTRIBUTION	6/10	YOUR RATING	/10

CLUBS SCHALKE 04, BAYERN MUNICH
COUNTRY GERMANY
CAPS 92+ **PEAK** 2011-2016
HONOURS WORLD CUP,
CHAMPIONS LEAGUE,
7 GERMAN LEAGUE TITLES

MANUEL NEUER

There have been **revolutionary** 'keepers before. Manchester United and Denmark legend Peter Schmeichel invented the **star-shape** save. Colombia's René Higuita came up with the **Scorpion** (check it out – still crazy even now).

Neuer has changed even more. He's brilliant on crosses and commands his area like a muscular king, but it's as **sweeper-keeper** – coming out of his area to **patrol the space** behind his defence – that he truly **rules.**

It **looks** risky. It doesn't **always** work. You'll have to watch out for his **constant appeals** to the ref for fouls and favours. But without Neuer's dash there's no 2014 World Cup win for Germany. There's no Ederson doing it for Man City, there's no Alisson doing it for Liverpool.

At that World Cup in Brazil, **Neuer finished the tournament with 244 passes.** Lionel Messi managed **242.** There's your case right there.

| SHOT STOPPING | 7/10 | COMMAND OF BOX | 9/10 | DISTRIBUTION | 10/10 | YOUR RATING | /10 |

CLUBS ATLETICO MADRID, MANCHESTER UNITED
COUNTRY SPAIN
CAPS 41+
PEAK 2014-2018
HONOURS FA CUP, ENGLISH LEAGUE TITLE, LEAGUE CUP, 2 EUROPA LEAGUES

DAVID DE GEA

People **ask questions** about De Gea. He's had a few **rough patches**, but all goalies do. He looks a bit **skinny** for a 'keeper, although so does Kepa Arrizabalaga. He used to **struggle** on crosses.

But with De Gea it's all about belief: his in himself, yours in him. If you can get him at his **best**, you have a 'keeper to build a team around. Five times he's won Match of the Day's **save of the season.** Three years in a row he won Manchester United's player of the year. His **reflexes** are unreal, his **positioning** spot-on every time.

And his **feet**, as befits a pure shot-stopper, are **sheer magic**. De Gea understands that it doesn't matter **how** you save them. Just **save** them. If that means studs, and toes, and ankles, that's just fine.

Don't listen to the doubters. De Gea knows and so should **you**. This is a 'keeper who can win you games.

SHOT STOPPING	COMMAND OF BOX	DISTRIBUTION	YOUR RATING
10/10	8/10	7/10	/10

MANAGER'S NOTES

1. What's the <u>priority</u> for your team: pure shot-stopper like Banks and De Gea, or sweeper-keeper like Neuer?

2. Would you take a great defensive organiser like Solo or Trautmann even if they're a harder character to manage?

3. Do you want a (tall) and dominating 'keeper like Buffon or someone (smaller) and more agile?

THE DECISION

Who is going to be the **goalkeeper** in your squad?
Draw them here, giving the trophy to your first choice,
and the medal to your second choice.
Don't forget to add their names to the silverware!

Every club needs a badge. And there are some absolute creative classics out there. Sheffield Wednesday's **owl** (because the area where the ground is built was originally known as Owlerton). West Ham's crossed **hammers.** Wolves', er, **wolf.**

What's your club's emblem going to be – a **bird** or **animal**? The **first letter of each word** in its name overlaid on each other (like Inter Milan – so cool)? Something that refers to its **nickname or origins**, like the gun of Arsenal, who got their name from a place where guns were made?

You could add a **star** for every major honour, as Juve have. A **motto** is always a nice touch, like Spurs' Latin one, 'Audere est Facere', ('To dare is to do'), or Liverpool's **'You'll never walk alone'**. Draw yours in the shield below.

BADGE

FORMATIONS

Now this is one of the most fun parts of a manager's job. But first you've got another decision to make. Are you a manager who wants to choose their **ideal formation** and then pick the players **to suit it?** If so, read this section now.

But if you prefer the idea of selecting **the top 11 players available** and then **choosing the formation** that will get the best out of them, you might be better off returning to this section once you've picked your team.

Either way, you've got a rock-solid basis to work with here, which gives you roughly a **4–4–2 traditional formation**:

Goalkeeper

Right-back • Centre-back: stopper • Centre-back: distributor • Left-back

Right midfield • Sitting midfielder • Attacking midfielder • Left midfield

Second striker • Finisher

But it's built with heaps of **flexibility** for you to set up your team exactly as you like and move things around depending on your players' strengths. Left- and right-sided full-backs, some who are **pure defenders**, others who love to **bomb on** and overlap, operating as wing-backs. One centre-back who can head and **tackle** all day long, another who can **drop deeper** to sweep or **step out** to play.

The wide midfielders could play **out on the wing**, hugging the touchline. They could **cut in** on their other foot, or **play right up** to be almost part of the front line. You could have your central midfielder to **sit a little deeper** and tackle, or to **create and run** all day. The other to look **forward**, to push on as far as you want them to. **It's up to you.**

One striker who can **hold the ball up** and play in a team-mate, another to **bury every chance** they're given. If you prefer one of them to drop deeper, you can. There are **options** here to play the way you choose, and players good enough to adjust to your *favourite* tactics.

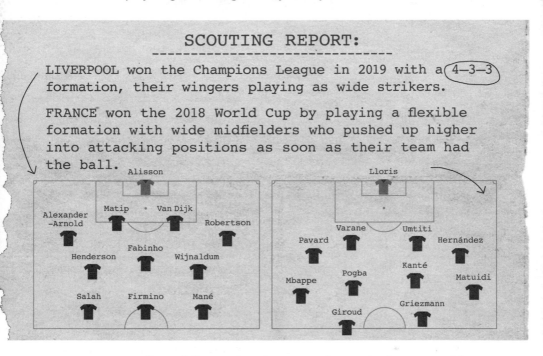

SCOUTING REPORT:

LIVERPOOL won the Champions League in 2019 with a 4—3—3 formation, their wingers playing as wide strikers.

FRANCE won the 2018 World Cup by playing a flexible formation with wide midfielders who pushed up higher into attacking positions as soon as their team had the ball.

Alisson

Lloris

Matip • Van Dijk

Alexander-Arnold

Robertson

Fabinho

Henderson

Wijnaldum

Salah   Firmino   Mané

Varane   Umtiti

Pavard

Hernández

Mbappe   Pogba   Kanté

Matuidi

Giroud   Griezmann

Draw your preferred formation here, and watch the opposition panic as they see what tactical wonders you have come up with.

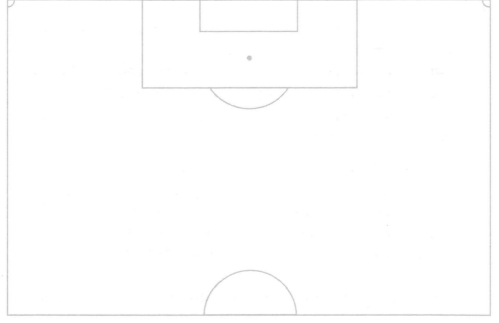

25

Right-backs used to be a bit dull.

You ended up on the right side of defence if you weren't quite skilful enough to be a winger, or dominant enough to be a centre-back. You ended up there because you were always reliably 7/10 but seldom more. You could defend but not much else.

Not any more. The best right-backs are now barely right-backs at all. They're on the right, but they can cut in. They're at the back, except when they're bombing forward. They can pass like midfielders, shoot from distance like cannons and cross like wing wonders.

You're a right-back because you can do it all.

And so this is a huge selection shout. You want someone with the energy and engine to get up and down the line all day. They have to work brilliantly with the centre-back inside them and the midfielder ahead of them.

They have to be able to tackle, head and stop flashy forwards in their tracks. Fitness is essential; most right-backs play most games a season. And they have to be strong characters – if you're away from home, you'll be within earshot of all those opposition fans along the touchline.

Good thing is, we've got some absolute beauties in the line-up. Let's get busy.

CLUBS BLACKPOOL
COUNTRY ENGLAND
CAPS 43 **PEAK** 1960-1964
HONOURS WORLD CUP

JIMMY ARMFIELD

Ah, lovely Jimmy . . . We'll get to his **skills** in a minute. But if you want a player who'll give you everything, who will **inspire** the team with his example, who will stay as **normal** as the fella next door even when he's the **greatest in the world?** You want **Jimmy.**

And did he have some skills. An England debut away in Brazil, in front of 120,000 fans at the epic Maracana stadium. Voted **best right-back** at the 1962 World Cup. Would have been best right-back at the 1966 World Cup had he not got **injured** at the worst possible time. Arsenal wanted to sign him. **And** Spurs. **And** Manchester United.

Of course they did – he was strong, fast, a player who could **see it all happening** in front of him before it actually did. But he **stayed** with his first club, Blackpool, because he knew they loved him and **he** loved them back, making **627 appearances** for them over a 17-year period.

Jimmy. Maybe the **nicest man** in football. And a **sensational** player too.

| PACE | 8/10 | TACKLING | 8/10 | COUNTER ATTACKING | 7/10 | YOUR RATING | /10 |

27

CLUBS FLUMINENSE, SANTOS, FLAMENGO, NEW YORK COSMOS

COUNTRY BRAZIL

CAPS 53   **PEAK** 1968-1972

HONOURS WORLD CUP

CARLOS ALBERTO

There's **so much** you can say about Carlos Alberto. He could **tackle** like a tank, **dribble** round opponents like they were traffic cones and **smash goals in** from all over the shop. When he **captained** Brazil at the 1970 World Cup they were maybe the best team of all time. The way he played balls into Pelé up front may tempt you to **pick them together again** in your team.

But why he would be such a **thriller** to have on your side is summed up by the goal he scored in that final of 1970. Striker Tostão **wins it**. Clodoaldo beats at least four Italian players. Rivellino pings it down the left, Jairzinho cuts inside, Pelé calls **just outside the box**, kills it, and hears the **shout.**

It's Carlos Alberto, **steaming up** on his outside like a runaway train. **Kaboom** – first-time hit, on the move, ball sizzling across the 'keeper and into the **far corner** of the net.

A goal you could watch **again and again**, from a right-back you could pick **every** time.

| PACE | **9/10** | TACKLING | **8/10** | COUNTER ATTACKING | **10/10** | YOUR RATING | /10 |

CLUBS SÃO PAULO, REAL ZARAGOZA, PALMEIRAS, ROMA, A.C. MILAN

COUNTRY BRAZIL

CAPS 142 **PEAK** 1998-2002

HONOURS BRAZILIAN CHAMPIONSHIP, 2 COPA LIBERTADORES, EUROPEAN CUP-WINNERS' CUP, 2 ITALIAN LEAGUE TITLES, CHAMPIONS LEAGUE, 2 WORLD CUPS, COPA AMÉRICA

CAFU

Brazil and right-backs. They just keep inspiring each other. Cafu was two weeks old when Carlos Alberto banged in that screamer in 1970. It was like the baby felt something magical in the air, **breathed it in** and made it his own.

His nickname in Italy was **Il Pendolino,** the Express Train. Not because he could carry 200 passengers but because he had **so much pace.** He was a legend at getting **dreamy crosses** in. Pick Cafu and you get a man who can **defend** but set up **goals** for others too.

You get the natural **leadership** of a man who captained his country. The **most capped Brazilian footballer** of all time, 21 games at World Cup finals, in the final three times, **winning it** twice. And you get a player who **smiled** no matter how bad things got, with a wonderful determination too. Before he achieved all those incredible things, Cafu was **rejected** by five different clubs as a kid.

He never gave up. And he'll **never** give up for you.

PACE	**9/10**	TACKLING	**6/10**	COUNTER ATTACKING	**10/10**	YOUR RATING	/10

CLUBS MONACO, PARMA, JUVENTUS, BARCELONA

COUNTRY FRANCE

CAPS 142 **PEAK** 1998-2002

HONOURS WORLD CUP, EUROPEAN CHAMPIONSHIP, 2 ITALIAN LEAGUE TITLES, FRENCH CUP, ITALIAN CUP, UEFA CUP

LILIAN THURAM

An amazing tackler, great in the air, a pure defender. But it's how he handles the **tough times** that makes Lilian such a smart pick.

Money was tight when he was a kid. The family had to **relocate** from the Caribbean to France. **His dad wasn't around.** But he was to become the **most expensive defender** in history when he moved from Parma to Juventus. And he still stayed chilled and **humble**.

You want it summed up in **one** game? It's France vs Croatia in the semi-finals of the 1998 World Cup. France – the hosts, the **favourites** – go **a goal down** when Thuram plays Croatia's striker onside.

That might have done for many. **Not this hero.** First, he sticks in a **big tackle** followed by a one-two and an **instinctive finish** for the equaliser. Then – off his **wrong** foot, his leftie – he curls an absolute **peach** into the far corner for the winner. Paris goes crazy. France go on to **win** their first World Cup. **Thuram just stays Thuram.**

| PACE | **8**/10 | TACKLING | **9**/10 | COUNTER ATTACKING | **8**/10 | YOUR RATING | /10 |

CLUBS TALLERES, BANFIELD, INTER MILAN
COUNTRY ARGENTINA
CAPS 143 **PEAK** 2002-2008
HONOURS 5 ITALIAN LEAGUE TITLES,
4 ITALIAN CUPS, CHAMPIONS LEAGUE, UEFA CUP

JAVIER ZANETTI

Don't be put off by the nickname. **'The Tractor'** isn't great. It's not **fair** either.

Oh, for sure, Zanetti had an amazing **engine**, and he could keep going all day. He could **tow** a team with him, and he was almost impossible to **get past**. Alright, he **was** actually a bit like a tractor. But it would have to be such an **elegant** tractor. One that looked so cool. And went as **fast** as a sports car.

Here's what else you're getting. **Massive loyalty: 858 appearances** for Inter Milan. A **natural leader:** 15 years as skipper, only **two** red cards in his entire career. **Total versatility:** he could play left-back or centre-mid just as easily as right-back.

There's **more**. No one **trained** as hard as Zanetti, which is one of the reasons he was **never** injured. Pick him and he'll play and play.

You can sum him up with his **hairstyle**. Always perfect. Never flashy, **never out of place.**

| PACE | 8/10 | TACKLING | 9/10 | COUNTER ATTACKING | 9/10 | YOUR RATING | /10 |

CLUBS BAHIA, SEVILLA, BARCELONA, JUVENTUS, PARIS SAINT-GERMAIN, SÃO PAULO

COUNTRY BRAZIL

CAPS 118+ **PEAK** 2010-2016

HONOURS 3 CHAMPIONS LEAGUES, 2 UEFA CUPS, 6 SPANISH LEAGUE TITLES, 5 SPANISH CUPS, ITALIAN LEAGUE TITLE, ITALIAN CUP, 2 FRENCH LEAGUE TITLES, FRENCH CUP, 2 COPA AMÉRICAS

DANI ALVES

So **Brazil** had Carlos Alberto, who was the best right-back of **his** era, and he inspired Cafu, who was the best right-back of **his** era, and then Cafu inspired Dani Alves, who turned out to be . . . **well, exactly**.

Unbelievable energy. The **attacking** style of a rampant winger. Great **crosser** of the ball, scorer of great **long-range goals.**

You'll need to play him with another defender who's happy to **cover** for him. Nothing is going to stop Dani Alves **going forward,** so you need to accept that, not least because it works: he's won **more major trophies** than **any** other player in history.

Play him at right-back and it's like having an **extra creative midfielder**, and not a selfish one. He set up an **insane** number of goals for Leo Messi at Barcelona. And he will never stop **trying** for you. Success, he always said, is giving your best. **His best is the best.**

PACE	9/10	TACKLING	5/10	COUNTER ATTACKING	10/10	YOUR RATING	/10

CLUBS ARSENAL, BIRMINGHAM CITY, BOSTON BREAKERS
COUNTRY ENGLAND
CAPS 140 **PEAK** 2010-2015
HONOURS CHAMPIONS LEAGUE,
6 ENGLISH LEAGUE TITLES, 7 FA CUPS,
5 LEAGUE CUPS

ALEX SCOTT

Alex has the **superstar status** to transform your team. **So many games at the top of international football**. Experience across the biggest leagues in the world. Trophies, oh so many **trophies . . .**

But here's the **big** thing. She learned her football on the **small cage pitch** on her estate. You **grow** your game there – players coming at you from **all sides,** no **time** on the ball, so little **space** – and you step out on a proper big pitch and you're suddenly the **boss** of everything around you. Now you've got time, because you've learned how to **create** it. You've got a **touch** that kills a ball on your toes. You can **turn** and lay the ball off and **find little angles** and a weight of **pass** that no one else can see and feel.

All the **magic ability** she would bring to your team – the **calm** reading of the game, the hard work, the **understanding** of what needs to happen next – comes from the **cage**. **Set her free.**

| PACE | 7/10 | TACKLING | 9/10 | COUNTER ATTACKING | 8/10 | YOUR RATING | /10 |

CLUBS SUNDERLAND, EVERTON, LIVERPOOL, MANCHESTER CITY, LYON

COUNTRY ENGLAND

CAPS 79+ **PEAK** 2016-

HONOURS 2 CHAMPIONS LEAGUES, 3 ENGLISH LEAGUE TITLES, FA CUP, LEAGUE CUP, 2 FRENCH LEAGUE TITLE, FRENCH CUP

LUCY BRONZE

We need to start with a couple of things about Lucy's name. First, there's nothing bronze about it. This woman is **gold standard** all the way through.

Secondly, her middle name is **Tough.** It's because that was her **mum's surname** before she got married. It should also be because **she is tough as nails**. You don't mess with Lucy Bronze, unless you want to get **messed with** seriously.

There's the tackling. There's the **strength**. There's the determination, and the **unreal fitness.** Bronze will **own** that side of the pitch for you, and stick the attackers in her back pocket. There's the established **relationships** – with Steph Houghton to her left for England, with Ada Hegerberg up front for Lyon. Link 'em up again and see them work **fresh miracles** for you.

And most of all, there's the **attitude.** Total **self-belief**, all of it justified. **There's no player like her.**

| PACE | 8/10 | TACKLING | 8/10 | COUNTER ATTACKING | 9/10 | YOUR RATING | /10 |

MANAGER'S NOTES

1. Do you want a defender first and foremost, like Jimmy Armfield, or an attacking machine like Dani Alves?

2. How much (pace) do you need? Is your right-winger going to provide the speed instead (go to page 78 to see what your options are)?

3. Right-backs are the ultimate team players. Who has the right character to bond your new unit?

THE DECISION

Who is going to be the **right-back** in your squad?
Draw them here, giving the trophy to your first choice,
and the medal to your second choice.
Don't forget to add their names to the silverware!

Look around at your mates. How many are right-footed? Okay. And how many are left-footed?

And that, in one simple sum, is why a top left-back is so valuable. They'll stop every attack coming down that side of the pitch, and there aren't many who can play there. Even if your right foot is an absolute wand you'll still need to look like a natural on your leftie to have a chance in this position, which makes each of our options here an absolute diamond of a footballer.

Different eras, different styles. We go all the way back to the middle of the last century and all the way through to the 'n' of the now, and each could bring something different and special to your team.

You'll want your left-back to have pace. Can't have them being skinned by a speedy winger. They'll have to tackle hard and with the sort of timing that leaves a striker wondering where on earth the ball went. They'll need the attacking skills to canter down that touchline in support of their team-mates when their team has the ball, and the stamina to keep doing it all day long.

Oh, and they've got to be able to link up with the centre-backs inside them. And they've got to be able to pass, because so many of the team's moves will start with them out wide and the ball at their feet. It sounds ridiculously hard. Luckily these eight legends made it look ridiculously easy.

CLUBS BOTAFOGO
COUNTRY BRAZIL
CAPS 75 **PEAK** 1958-1962
HONOURS 2 WORLD CUPS, SOUTH AMERICAN CHAMPIONSHIP

NILTON SANTOS

What a player . . . Nilton Santos was maybe the **first attacking full-back** of all time. No one had really thought a defender should do **more** than just defend, understandably when they're literally called **'defender'**. But it came **naturally** to him, and **what a sight** he could be in your team – **cheeky** step-overs, **ice-cool** under pressure, all the tackling stuff but **so much more**. It drove a few managers mad. **They** weren't used to it. You would be.

You'd also get all the knowledge and **insight** you'd expect from a bloke whose nickname was **The Encyclopedia,** the experience of someone whose displays helped Brazil win the 1958 and 1962 World Cups and the **consistency** of a player who made more than **700 club appearances**.

One tip: maybe **don't** pick him if you're also going to pick **Stanley Matthews** on the right of midfield. Stan destroyed him when England **beat** Brazil 4–2. But if you're thinking about the **brilliant** Garrincha out there, well . . . they played together for club and country. **Beautifully.**

| PACE | 8/10 | TACKLING | 7/10 | COUNTER ATTACKING | 9/10 | YOUR RATING | /10 |

CLUBS INTER MILAN
COUNTRY ITALY
CAPS 94 **PEAK** 1967-1971
HONOURS
EUROPEAN CHAMPIONSHIP,
2 EUROPEAN CUPS, 4 ITALIAN LEAGUE
TITLES, ITALIAN CUP

GIACINTO FACCHETTI

Giacinto was such a **strong** player that going round him was like **trying to go round a wall**. So **commanding** that you could launch balls at his head or wingers at his feet and he'd **send them packing** all day long. **Passing out** from the back like he had **all the time in the world**, because with his touch he did.

In his Inter kit – broad blue and black stripes – he looked **sensational. Tall**, but able to **overlap** down the wing all day long. A **leader** for you who captained Italy 70 times and made 629 appearances for his club, able to switch to **sweeper** if he had to.

He's not going to give you any trouble. In all those years he was **sent off only once**, which is pretty amazing for a no-nonsense Italian defender. But he might give you **goals** – no defender in Italian league history has **ever scored more**.

Inter **retired his number 3 shirt** when he died. **They knew. We know.**

| PACE | 7/10 | TACKLING | 8/10 | COUNTER ATTACKING | 8/10 | YOUR RATING | /10 |

CLUBS BAYERN MUNICH, REAL MADRID, EINTRACHT BRAUNSCHWEIG

COUNTRY WEST GERMANY

CAPS 48 **PEAK** 1977-1981

HONOURS WORLD CUP, EUROPEAN CHAMPIONSHIP, EUROPEAN CUP, 5 GERMAN LEAGUE TITLES, 2 GERMAN CUPS, 2 SPANISH LEAGUE TITLES, SPANISH CUP

PAUL BREITNER

Now. You're going to get a lot of attitude with Breitner. He had a lot of big views on a lot of big things, and he liked sharing them **all** with his managers. He didn't like national anthems. Don't expect him to lead the **singing** on the bus.

You're also going to get a lot of hair. Breitner had so much of it on his head that he looked like a **mad German bush.**

But a **cool** bush. When he was running about with socks round his ankles, **perfectly balanced**, rampaging forward and **knocking** passes about with **either foot** – well, there was no one quite like him.

He **scored** in two different World Cup finals. He linked up an absolute treat with Franz Beckenbauer, which gives you another **potential peach of a pairing** at the back. And he made playing left-back look like the **best** position on the pitch, mainly because he was **so energetic and skilful** it looked like he was playing in **every** position anyway.

PACE **9/10**   TACKLING **7/10**   COUNTER ATTACKING **9/10**   YOUR RATING **/10**

CLUBS AJAX, VANCOUVER WHITECAPS, NAPOLI, CANNES

COUNTRY THE NETHERLANDS

CAPS 83 **PEAK** 1972-1976

HONOURS 3 EUROPEAN CUPS, 6 DUTCH LEAGUE TITLES, 4 DUTCH CUPS

RUUD KROL

There was something extraordinary about the Dutch teams of the 1970s. At a time when you were meant to stay in **one position** and do one thing, Ruud and his boys went everywhere and did **everything**. They called it **Total Football,** not least because they were totally **awesome.**

Ruud was so good with his right foot he **could** have played right-back. Whatever happens in your team **he'll be able to cope**. If you get injuries elsewhere and need someone who can **fill in** like a natural, Ruud's your man again. It's like getting **ten players in one.**

There'll be **goals.** Check out the one he **smashed in** from the edge of the box against Argentina in 1974. There'll be devastating passing. Check out the ball he **whipped in** from the left for Johan Cruyff's side-foot volley against Brazil at that same World Cup.

You don't **technically** have to pick him and Cruyff together. It would just be a **shameful waste** if you didn't, like toast without butter, or a cone without the ice-cream. **Exactly.**

PACE	7/10	TACKLING	7/10	COUNTER ATTACKING	10/10	YOUR RATING	/10

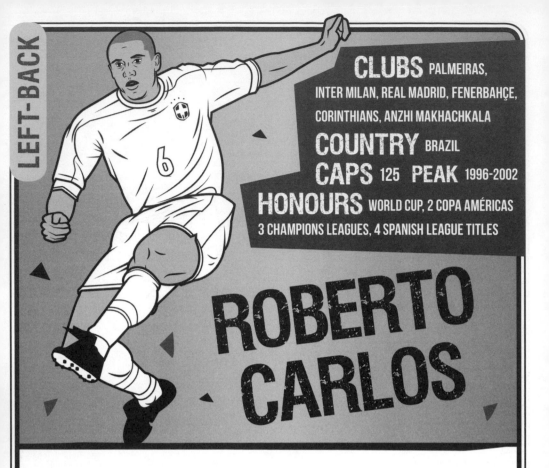

CLUBS PALMEIRAS, INTER MILAN, REAL MADRID, FENERBAHÇE, CORINTHIANS, ANZHI MAKHACHKALA
COUNTRY BRAZIL
CAPS 125 **PEAK** 1996-2002
HONOURS WORLD CUP, 2 COPA AMÉRICAS 3 CHAMPIONS LEAGUES, 4 SPANISH LEAGUE TITLES

ROBERTO CARLOS

There's a video on YouTube called **'Roberto Carlos Top 10 Crazy Goals That Shocked The World'**. That's entirely fair, because Roberto Carlos scored some **truly crazy goals.** One from pretty much the **corner-flag** for Real Madrid against Tenerife. One for Brazil against France in 1997 that might just be the **greatest** free-kick of all time. Basically, pick Roberto Carlos and **you're getting goals.**

But there **also** needs to be a video called 'Roberto Carlos Top 10 Crazy **Runs Down The Wing'**. And another one called 'Roberto Carlos Top 10 Crazy Times He **Tackled A Winger And Made Him Cry'**. **That's what he's doing for you.** And, since he was part of the same Real team of superstar **galacticos** as Zinedine Zidane and David Beckham, he's already got a **relationship** there that you can cash in on once again.

Oh – he also had the **biggest thighs** in football. **That's** where the goal power came from. And the runs. And the stamina. You'd have noticed anyway, but still. They were **MASSIVE.**

PACE	**9/10**	TACKLING	**6/10**	COUNTER ATTACKING	**10/10**	YOUR RATING	**/10**

CLUBS A.C. MILAN
COUNTRY ITALY
CAPS 126 **PEAK** 1994-2003
HONOURS 5 EUROPEAN CUPS/
CHAMPIONS LEAGUES, 7 ITALIAN LEAGUE
TITLES, ITALIAN CUP

PAOLO MALDINI

The **numbers** for Maldini are so good they could make you **dizzy**. A first-team debut for Milan **aged 16**. A regular at 17. A regular for **another 24 years**. A massive **902 appearances** for Milan and 14 years of international football with Italy. Eight Champions League finals. **Eight!** Oh, you're getting **magic stats**, alright. But numbers can't tell you everything.

They can't tell you about his **elegance,** about how he tackled opponents before they even knew it was **happening,** about how he didn't even **need** to make some tackles because he **took** the ball before it got that far. They can't tell you about his **positioning**, about his **man-marking**, about a right foot that was as good as his left. They can't tell you, as Zlatan and Ronaldo could, that he was the greatest defender either of them **ever** played against.

One more thought for you. He was **supreme** alongside Franco Baresi and Fabio Cannavaro at centre-back and Cafu at right-back. You could do **a lot worse** than linking those **beauties** up again.

| PACE | 810 | TACKLING | 10/10 | COUNTER ATTACKING | 9/10 | YOUR RATING | /10 |

CLUBS BAYERN MUNICH, STUTTGART
COUNTRY GERMANY
CAPS 113 **PEAK** 2006-2010
HONOURS WORLD CUP,
CHAMPIONS LEAGUE, 8 GERMAN LEAGUE
TITLES, 6 GERMAN CUPS

PHILIPP LAHM

Lahm had one of those **nicknames you can't forget: the Magic Dwarf.** He wasn't tall. But clearly, if they're calling you magic, you're **pretty** special.

And Lahm was. He'll bring you pace, touch, all manner of **lovely passing**. Goals, too, like the **right-footed curler** he bent in to become the first goal-scorer of the 2006 World Cup. He lifted the World Cup as **Germany's captain** in 2014 having played both right back and centre midfield, but don't think he's **wasted** at left-back. He just ran the game from **there** instead.

Lahm's not flashy. He's not about fast cars and big nights out. He's not going to give you any **trouble**. He will, however, give the right-sided opposition players absolute **nightmares.** Need a recommendation from a decent fellow manager? Pep Guardiola described him as the **most intelligent** player he ever coached. That's **big chat**.

Oh yeah. He's not even that small. At 5ft 7in (1.7m) he's the **same height** as Leo Messi. **Fact.**

| PACE | 8/10 | TACKLING | 8/10 | COUNTER ATTACKING | 9/10 | YOUR RATING | /10 |

CLUBS QUEEN'S PARK, DUNDEE UNITED, HULL CITY, LIVERPOOL

COUNTRY SCOTLAND

CAPS 34+ **PEAK** 2018-

HONOURS CHAMPIONS LEAGUE

ANDY ROBERTSON

Tricky one, this. There's a very good case for **Ashley Cole** being one of your options (107 caps for England, seven FA Cup wins, one Champions League, three Premier League titles). Robertson, by comparison, is only just **getting started**. In 2016 he was still playing in the **Championship** for Hull.

And yet. The **sweetness** of that left peg. The **relentless** running. The covering at the back, the passing, the pressing, the absolutely **ridiculous** number of chances he **sets up** for his Liverpool team-mates.

If you want **young talent**, if you want to watch a player start brilliant and then **get even better** under your coaching and management, Robertson could be your man. If you're picking Mo Salah up front or Virgil van Dijk at the back, why wouldn't you **also** pick someone who plays off them so wonderfully well? Celtic **released** Robertson when he was 15 for being too small. Since then he's grown into one of the most exciting full-backs **in the world**. **Is it time to give him the chance to shine?**

PACE	9/10	TACKLING	7/10	COUNTER ATTACKING	10/10	YOUR RATING	/10

MANAGER'S NOTES

1. Are you looking for a **natural** left-footer like Robbo, or a right-footer <u>converted across</u> like Krol or Lahm?

2. Are you choosing them for their (skills alone,) or for the way they might **link up** with your other picks?

3. There's a **seven-inch** difference in height between our biggest player and smallest. What matters more to you – having a player who can take set-pieces, or one who can <u>defend</u> them?

THE DECISION

Who is going to be the **left-back** in your squad?
Draw them here, giving the trophy to your first choice,
and the medal to your second choice.
Don't forget to add their names to the silverware!

PRE-MATCH MEAL

To perform at their best, your **magnificent** team are going to need the right **fuel** before a big match.

In the old days this was straightforward: a massive plate of **steak and chips**. Tasty, maybe, but so heavy in your stomach that it must have been like running about with a **cannonball** stuffed up your shirt. Some players even smashed down a couple of **raw eggs** as a sort of disgusting sloppy drink. **Shocker.**

By the 1990s it was **healthier** if more boring. Big bowl of pasta, no sauce, grilled chicken, **no sauce**. Players ate it because they felt they **had** to, rather than because they wanted to.

Butter was banned. **Tomato ketchup** was banned. **Nightmare.**

Now there is the **new normal** – slightly less pasta, maybe some quinoa, **definitely** some sushi. But there are still **mavericks.** Gareth Bale swears by baked beans on toast. Jamie Vardy has **three cans of Red Bull and a ham and cheese omelette.**

Luckily, you're the boss.

You decide everything with this team. **Stick your chef's hat on and draw your menu** and meal here.

Menu

RITUALS

We've all got our own way of getting ready for big games. Little routines, **strange superstitions**. Something that makes us feel **lucky**, something that takes our mind off that mouthy opposition manager or their lightning striker for a bit.

Sometimes they work.
Sometimes they're madness.

Pop down your own ideas and see what works for you. With a little help from other famous footballing names from down the years.

Cheeky wees

There's no nice way of saying this, but former Argentina goalie Sergio Goycochea got into a habit of weeing on the pitch before penalty shoot-outs at the 1990 World Cup. Not very lucky for the player who had to run through the wee-patch, was it?

Last man out of changing-room

Former Manchester United and England star Paul Ince was a big fan of this one. It made him feel like the boss. Trouble is, what happens if you get two players who both want to be last one out? Awks.

Lucky pants

Old favourite, this one. You wear the pants, your team wins. You wear the pants again, they win again. The pants start stinking, because they're dirty. You don't care, because they're lucky. Your players do, because of the smell.

Not shooting before a game

Gary Lineker would refuse to take any practice shots. Apparently he was worried about using up goals. Work that one out.

My Pre-match Ritual

The thing about a stopper is that you know what their job is.

Stopping things. Stopping strikers. Stopping chances. Stopping balls, passes and movement. Stopping everything they can. In two words: a pure defender.

This doesn't mean they don't have skills. To be able to stop stuff you have to be in the right place, and you don't get in the right place by accident.

To be able to man-mark you have to be able to run as fast as the striker you're marking, twist with them, turn with them.

To be able to tackle you have to be capable of timing your challenge as sweetly as that striker would like to time their shot. The shot that you're going to stop.

And so the following are among the greatest players of all time. One of them will be the rock that your team will be built on.

Hard. Lumpy. And stopping everything that tries to get past.

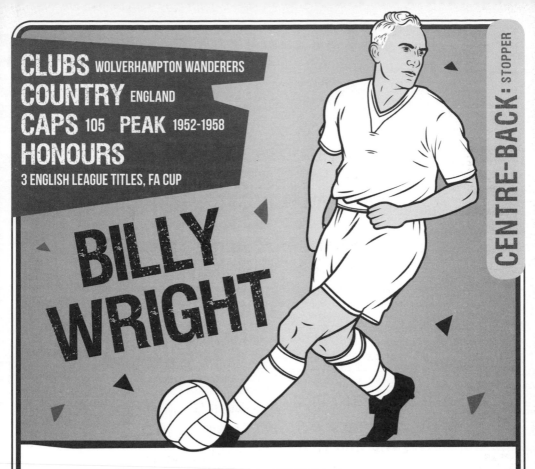

CLUBS WOLVERHAMPTON WANDERERS
COUNTRY ENGLAND
CAPS 105 **PEAK** 1952-1958
HONOURS
3 ENGLISH LEAGUE TITLES, FA CUP

BILLY WRIGHT

His shorts went down to his knees. His shirt was as baggy as a tent, and **twice** as heavy. And yet Billy Wright was the first **superstar style icon** of a central defender. Always in the right place. Never panicked. The **first player** in international football history **to win 100 caps**. Married to a **famous singer**. Billy Wright was David Beckham before David Beckham was even **born**.

You're getting **enormous determination** with Billy. When he was 15, he was told he was **too small** to make it as a professional. A couple of years later he **broke his ankle so badly** he was told that he'd never come back. He **proved everyone wrong** with 541 appearances for Wolves. In all those appearances and tackles he was **never booked once**.

A huge jump, a thumping header of the ball. A **captain** who made all his players want to win for him, and so much **modesty** than he would probably argue with all the above. The Wright choice. **In every way.**

| TACKLING | 9/10 | HEADING | 8/10 | MARKING | 8/10 | YOUR RATING | /10 |

CLUBS VARESE, JUVENTUS, FIORENTINA, PIACENZA
COUNTRY ITALY
CAPS 71 **PEAK** 1978-1982
HONOURS WORLD CUP, UEFA CUP, EUROPEAN CUP-WINNERS' CUP, 6 ITALIAN LEAGUE TITLES, 2 ITALIAN CUPS

CLAUDIO GENTILE

There was absolutely nothing gentle about Gentile. A more accurate name for him would have been Claudio **Nasti**. No one **tackled** like Claudio. Not as often, or as effectively, or with such **enjoyment**.

Select him at the heart of your defence and he'll **scare** the opposition strikers so badly they'll be having **nightmares** about him for weeks. When Italy played Argentina at the 1982 World Cup, Gentile fouled the normally **unstoppable** Diego Maradona 11 times in the first half, then fouled him 12 times in the second. That's a foul every four minutes. **'Football is not for ballerinas!'** Claudio cackled afterwards.

Italy won. **And that's the thing** – the Gentile touch **worked.** He was only actually sent off **once** in his career, and that was for two yellows, the second after a handball.

Pair him with his Italy and Juve team-mate Gaetano Scirea and you get the **perfect** balance between **good** and **evil.**

| TACKLING | 10/10 | HEADING | 8/10 | MARKING | 10/10 | YOUR RATING | /10 |

CLUBS SAN DIEGO SPIRIT
COUNTRY USA
CAPS 239 **PEAK** 1995-1999
HONOURS 2 WORLD CUPS,
2 OLYMPIC GOLDS

JOY FAWCETT

**Not sure we can start anywhere else apart from that number of caps: 241.
241!** That's **twice** as many as Wayne Rooney. It's three times as many as Gary Lineker.
It's **five** times as many as Harry Kane (for now).

So Joy would bring **crazy experience** to your line-up. There is no big-game atmosphere that
she wouldn't be able to handle; when you've played **every single minute of three
World Cups in a row,** you've seen it all and dealt with **everything**.

For someone who did such a **remarkable** job at stopping strikers, she never resorted to
any nasty business, keeping it as clean as the **Queen**. Not a single red card in **all** those
international appearances, only two yellow cards. It's like Sergio Ramos in reverse.

What's that? You want goals at the other end? Not a problem. Joy came up with
27 for the national side, including an absolutely **critical** one in the big quarter-final win
over Germany at the 1999 World Cup.

| TACKLING | 8/10 | HEADING | 8/10 | MARKING | 8/10 | YOUR RATING | /10 |

CLUBS NAPOLI, PARMA, INTER MILAN, JUVENTUS, REAL MADRID

COUNTRY ITALY

CAPS 136 **PEAK** 2004-2008

HONOURS WORLD CUP, UEFA CUP, 2 SPANISH LEAGUE TITLES, 2 ITALIAN CUPS

FABIO CANNAVARO

Defenders don't tend to win **World Player of the Year.** The judges' eyes are too often drawn to **flashy skills** and **big goals.**

So the fact that **Fabio won it in 2006** tells you **how good** he was. And he was amazing in that year's World Cup, when the defence he led **conceded only two goals** – one a penalty, the other an own-goal – **in 690 minutes** played across seven games.

When he lifted the **trophy** at the end of that tournament in Germany, the Italian supporters called him '**Il Muro di Berlino**' (The Berlin Wall) because he was so hard to **get past**. Remarkable pace and positional sense, a **huge** leap.

He was **calm**, he loved to organise those around him. **And boy could he tackle . . .** As a youngster at Napoli he **slid in ferociously** on Maradona. The coaches kicked off, telling him to leave the superstar alone. Maradona told him to carry on. **He knew talent** when he felt it **booting him up in the air.**

| TACKLING | **10**/10 | HEADING | **8**/10 | MARKING | **9**/10 | YOUR RATING | /10 |

CLUBS NANTES, MARSEILLE, A.C. MILAN, CHELSEA
COUNTRY FRANCE
CAPS 116 **PEAK** 1996-2000
HONOURS WORLD CUP, EUROPEAN CHAMPIONSHIP, 2 CHAMPIONS LEAGUES, 2 ITALIAN LEAGUE TITLES, FA CUP

MARCEL DESAILLY

What a classy act. Strong in the air, a supreme tackler. The technique and passing skills to play centre-mid or sweeper if required, the **fitness** to keep going all day long.

That Milan team he won the Champions League with was **special**. The France team he was part of that won the World Cup was **even better**.

Desailly kept **improving** as he kept **moving**. When he went to Chelsea, he somehow became **even more powerful**, despite having been as strong as **Mr Incredible** beforehand. Good news for the Blues, very bad news for Premier League strikers.

As a TV pundit he could **spot things** others couldn't. Use that **insight** and your team's tactics will get a huge boost. As a man he was always **upbeat** and enthusiastic. His **laugh** might be the most glorious in football history. Use that around the team and your dressing-room will be **a happy place**.

| TACKLING | 9/10 | HEADING | 7/10 | MARKING | 8/10 | YOUR RATING | /10 |

CLUBS ANDERLECHT, HAMBURG, MANCHESTER CITY
COUNTRY BELGIUM
CAPS 89 **PEAK** 2010-2014
HONOURS 4 ENGLISH LEAGUE TITLES,
2 FA CUPS, 4 LEAGUE CUPS, 2 BELGIAN LEAGUE TITLES

VINCENT KOMPANY

There's a decent case for saying that Kompany was Man City's **best signing ever.** That's not to knock the **marvels** of Agüero, Silva, De Bruyne and Sterling. It's just that Vincent was the difference between the old City – flaky, **flawed**, often close but never all the way – and the **new** one which would **dominate** English football for the next 10 years.

Kompany comes in and City win the FA Cup. He captains them to their first league title in **44 years**. He scores **priceless** goals in title-deciding games and he **mops up** in his own penalty box like a giant human sponge.

And so this is the menu if you choose this **inspirational** option. Amazing **strength** in the air. Great positioning. **Muscle** in the challenge, a leader who does it from the **front**.

A player who will take your **tactics** and **attitude** and make them **real** on the field of play. Someone everyone can **trust**, who fell so in love with Manchester that he even **married a City supporter. Swoony.**

| TACKLING | 9/10 | HEADING | 10/10 | MARKING | 8/10 | YOUR RATING | /10 |

CLUBS SEVILLA, REAL MADRID
COUNTRY SPAIN
CAPS 170+ **PEAK** 2008-2012
HONOURS WORLD CUP,
2 EUROPEAN CHAMPIONSHIPS, 4 CHAMPIONS LEAGUES,
4 SPANISH LEAGUE TITLES, 2 SPANISH CUPS

SERGIO RAMOS

So, the good news first. **Ramos is so fast,** so strong in the air, so good at bringing the ball out. He scores an **insane amount of goals** for a defender – **one every seven games on average** for Real, 21 in total for Spain. He's won **everything** you could want to win, and he's even got rid of the **bad hair** (long, lank, bit of string holding it back) too.

But. Massive but. The fouls. The sneakiness. The diving . . .

No one else in **history** has been shown **more yellow and red cards** in the Spanish league, or Champions League. The fact he's **never been sent off** in more than 170 appearances for **Spain** is an actual football **miracle**.

Maybe **you** can be the manager to get all the magic out of Ramos **without** the unpleasant stuff. Maybe you can stop him **kicking people**, or **falling over** when he's barely been touched, or **doing the dirty** on opposition players like he did to Liverpool's Mo Salah in the Champions League final of 2018. **Maybe.**

TACKLING	9/10	HEADING	8/10	MARKING	9/10

YOUR RATING /10

CLUBS GRONINGEN, CELTIC, SOUTHAMPTON, LIVERPOOL

COUNTRY THE NETHERLANDS

CAPS 32+ **PEAK** 2017-

HONOURS CHAMPIONS LEAGUE, 2 SCOTTISH LEAGUE TITLES, SCOTTISH LEAGUE CUP

VIRGIL VAN DIJK

There's a weird thing you see so often when Virgil van Dijk is in control of the ball: strikers **falling over**, or lying on the ground, or just looking totally **baffled**. At first it doesn't make sense. **What has happened to these fabulous players** who usually possess such balance, pace and control?

Then you realise. Virgil van Dijk has happened to them. He's **overpowered** them. Or **outpaced** them. Or **nicked** the ball off them at the **exact point** they thought it was theirs.

Sometimes he's overpowered them having **outpaced** them just before he nicks the ball off them. **That's how dominant he is.**

What a player to have at your disposal! Tall, **crazy pace** when it barely looks like he's jogging, never ever harried or hustled. **So smooth.** So devastating for strikers. And he's **still getting better.**

TACKLING	HEADING	MARKING	YOUR RATING
10/10	9/10	9/10	/10

MANAGER'S NOTES

1. It's a tricky <u>balance</u> between hard and fair – is your pick at risk of a **red card**, leaving you a player down?

2. **Great captains** are often found in the middle of the defence – are you going to want your captain here?

3. Defenders work in (pairs), or as a **unit**. Is it worth linking up **old team-mates** once again at the heart of your defence?

THE DECISION

Who is going to be the **stopper** in your squad?
Draw them here, giving the trophy to your first choice,
and the medal to your second choice.
Don't forget to add their names to the silverware!

Defenders defend. Which means the ones who can do all that and then a whole lot more – pass it out like creative midfielders, step out of defence with the ball like the perfect link between the back of the team and the front – are a special breed.

It's a hard job, making all that look so easy. But the great ball-players and sweepers do that. They're usually elegant, often tall and always beautifully comfortable on the ball. They can pass the ball off either foot, and have that sort of glorious pace where they're faster than anyone else without really looking like they're doing more than jogging.

But there's variety in there too. Sweepers tend to sit in behind the defence and do all the clearing up, spotting trouble before it happens, gliding over to make interceptions and snuff out the sparks before they become a fire.

Some use that extra time and space to fire dreamy balls to team-mates out wide or in their own little pocket of space in the middle. Some play closer to the other centre-back but have the technique and vision to move into midfield with or without the ball when the chance comes.

Decide what works for you. But feel good about it, whichever way you go, because the eight players up for selection are absolute bangers.

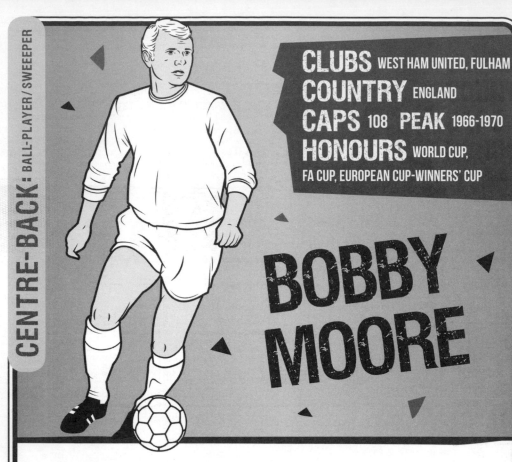

CLUBS WEST HAM UNITED, FULHAM
COUNTRY ENGLAND
CAPS 108 **PEAK** 1966-1970
HONOURS WORLD CUP,
FA CUP, EUROPEAN CUP-WINNERS' CUP

BOBBY MOORE

The best England player of all time? It's an easy argument to make. No one was like Bobby Moore before. **No one's been quite like him since.**

The big stuff. Moore was **captain** when England won **their only World Cup** and he was everything that was **great** about that team: modest, classy, **heroic.** Manager Alf Ramsey said England would never have won the World Cup without him. It was **his** quick free-kick that led to England's first goal and **his** calm pass out from the back that led to number four. In between, he **bossed it** at the back in the **stylish way** he always did.

Moore always **looked** great. In the red or white of England he made the shirt **iconic.** On the pitch he took what was expected of a defender and **transformed it** into something **magnificent.** His tackle on Jairzinho when England played Brazil at the 1970 World Cup might be the **greatest tackle** of all time.

You keep coming back to that same word with Bobby. The best.

| DOMINANCE 8/10 | DISTRIBUTION 8/10 | READING OF GAME 10/10 | YOUR RATING /10 |

CLUBS BAYERN MUNICH, NEW YORK COSMOS, HAMBURG

COUNTRY WEST GERMANY

CAPS 103 **PEAK** 1970-1975

HONOURS WORLD CUP, EUROPEAN CHAMPIONSHIP, 3 EUROPEAN CUPS, EUROPEAN CUP-WINNERS' CUP, 5 GERMAN LEAGUE TITLES, 4 GERMAN CUPS, 3 US TITLES

FRANZ BECKENBAUER

So Beckenbauer **watched** what Bobby Moore did, added **his own special talents** and touches and kicked it on. While always remaining **in total control**. They called him **Der Kaiser** (The Emperor), so you can guess how much incredible **leadership** he's bringing you. So much **trophy-winning** experience too – a World Cup, European Cups, league titles. Whatever contest or trouble your team might find itself in, he will have got through bigger and **nastier.**

There are the **skills** on the ball that come from someone who **began as a rampaging centre-midfielder**, the goals that come from a player as happy in and around his **opponents' box** as his own; **94 strikes** in 709 career appearances.

There's the **bravery** of a man who dislocated his shoulder in a World Cup semi, **strapped the ruined arm to his chest** with tape and played on. He can **sweep.** He can step out. He can defend, and attack, and lead. **Truly, Franz could do it all.**

DOMINANCE **9/10**   DISTRIBUTION **9/10**   READING OF GAME **9/10**   YOUR RATING **/10**

CLUBS SARMIENTO, RIVER PLATE, FIORENTINA, INTER MILAN
COUNTRY ARGENTINA
CAPS 70 **PEAK** 1978-1982
HONOURS 2 WORLD CUPS, 6 ARGENTINE LEAGUE TITLES

DANIEL PASSARELLA

Warning: Passarella is a hard man. You're going to have to pick him with the **right** team-mates. If anyone was **ever late** to training or team meetings he would go **bananas.** When he managed Argentina years later, he **banned** any players who had long hair.

And yet. Small, for a centre-back, at 5ft 8in (1.73m), but so good at **heading** the ball away that Diego Maradona said he was the **best** header of a football in history.

His left foot was a **wand** and it was a **weapon**. Endless **lunging** interceptions, so many free-kicks stuck top bins or **thundered** into the net in a way that left **scorched grass** in its wake.

He organised those around him **so relentlessly** that he'd be doing half your job for you. **'El Gran Capitán'** (the Great Captain) they called him when he led Argentina to the 1978 World Cup. They **knew** what they were talking about.

DOMINANCE **10/10** DISTRIBUTION **8/10** READING OF GAME **8/10** YOUR RATING **/10**

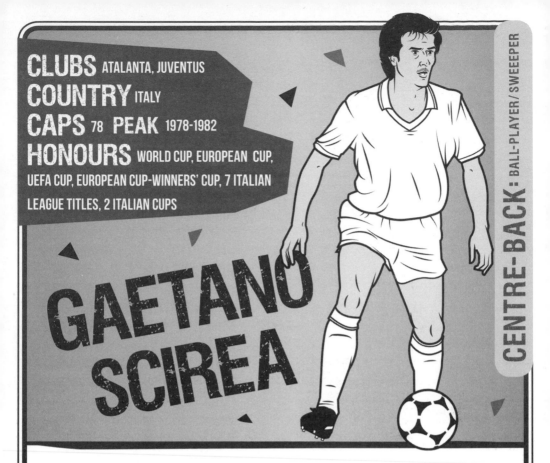

CLUBS ATALANTA, JUVENTUS
COUNTRY ITALY
CAPS 78 **PEAK** 1978-1982
HONOURS WORLD CUP, EUROPEAN CUP, UEFA CUP, EUROPEAN CUP-WINNERS' CUP, 7 ITALIAN LEAGUE TITLES, 2 ITALIAN CUPS

GAETANO SCIREA

CENTRE-BACK: BALL-PLAYER/SWEEPER

If this position in your team is not only about **substance** but also **style** (which it is, or **should** be), let's start with a mental image of Scirea at his best.

Tall. Black hair. The brilliant blue of the Italy World Cup '82 shirt. White shorts with a blue '7' on the left leg. Striding upfield with the ball **on his toes**, striker lying **baffled** on the ground behind him. Team-mates making all sorts of runs ahead of him, knowing the **perfect pass** could be coming their way.

What's that? He's **playing for Juve** rather than the national side? Okay. **All of the above,** except this time in broad black and white stripes that are **just** as classically cool.

Select Scirea and cash in on that **range of passing,** long and short. Benefit from **all that composure** on the ball, the reading of the game that gets a defender to a through-ball **milliseconds** before the forward. And the self-discipline that meant he was **never** sent off in his career.

DOMINANCE **9/10**   DISTRIBUTION **10/10**   READING OF GAME **9/10**   YOUR RATING **/10**

CLUBS A.C. MILAN
COUNTRY ITALY
CAPS 81 **PEAK** 1988-1993
HONOURS WORLD CUP, 3 EUROPEAN CUPS/CHAMPIONS LEAGUES, 6 ITALIAN LEAGUE TITLES

FRANCO BARESI

Scirea finished with Italy and Baresi took over. **Maybe he did it even better. Maybe.** The **style** was different. **Scruffier** rather than smart. Curly hair sticking up all over, usually **hairy-faced** as if he'd lost his razor, baggy shirt often **untucked.**

The class was unmistakeable. The pace of a hungry cheetah, the way he would **chase down** strikers and nip past them to win the ball! The **vision** to see what was about to happen long before any opponent, as if he were wearing **weird goggles** that allowed him to **see into the future.**

All sorts of **combinations** for your team open up with Franco. He had Paolo Maldini outside him at left-back for Italy, and handed over the captain's armband **having led Italy for 10 years** (respect). With Milan he **ruled Europe** behind midfielder Frank Rijkaard and striker Marco van Basten. With Baresi in your defence you're going to spend long periods as a manager actually feeling **quite relaxed.** He's **that** commanding. Just don't look at the other manager. He'll be looking sick.

DOMINANCE **10/10** DISTRIBUTION **8/10** READING OF GAME **9/10** YOUR RATING **/10**

CLUBS GRONINGEN, AJAX, PSV, BARCELONA, FEYENOORD
COUNTRY THE NETHERLANDS
CAPS 78 **PEAK** 1988-1992
HONOURS EUROPEAN CHAMPIONSHIP, 2 EUROPEAN CUPS, 4 SPANISH LEAGUE TITLES, SPANISH CUP, 4 DUTCH LEAGUE TITLES, 3 DUTCH CUPS

RONALD KOEMAN

CENTRE-BACK: BALL-PLAYER / SWEEEPER

Here's a clip to search out on YouTube. It comes under 'Ronald Koeman goals', like many, many others. You'll know it when you've found it. **Barca vs Trabzonspor,** Koeman advancing at the defence, the defence advancing at him. **Dink**. One chip over four defenders. Suddenly **through on goal**. 'Keeper coming out. **Dink** number 2. **Goal.**

The **Double-Dink** is a sensational finish. And Koeman, for a defender, was full of them – **blistering** free-kicks, including one against England that helped get manager Graham Taylor the sack. It was his **hammer** of a free-kick that won Barcelona their first European Cup. Only Leo Messi has scored more **penalties** for Barca. Only Messi has scored more **free-kicks**.

And that's just the goals. The same rocket-blaster of a right foot was just as good at **launching long-range passes** from his position behind the Barca or Dutch defence. And he steamed around his own half like a short, blond-haired king. **Useful note:** he played in the same Barca side as Pep Guardiola. So if **Pep's** going to be your assistant coach . . .

DOMINANCE **8/10** DISTRIBUTION **10/10** READING OF GAME **8/10** YOUR RATING **/10**

CLUBS WEST HAM UNITED, LEEDS UNITED, MANCHESTER UNITED, QUEENS PARK RANGERS

COUNTRY ENGLAND

CAPS 81 **PEAK** 2002-2008

HONOURS CHAMPIONS LEAGUE, 6 ENGLISH LEAGUE TITLES, 2 LEAGUE CUPS

RIO FERDINAND

For years **England supporters** had watched Italy, and Germany, and the Netherlands, and **almost everyone else**, enjoy the benefits of having a **ball-playing centre-back**. There was Bobby Moore and then there was no one else who could compare for a **very long** time.

Rio came along and **suddenly all was well in the world.** You could tell he started out as a **midfielder**, although you might not have known that he **sulked for three weeks** when he was first told to use those skills in **central defence** instead.

With Rio at the heart of it all your team will have the **best** of what a centre-back of this type can be. **Effortless pace** to close players and space down. Coming across or out to make tackles with the **sweetest of timing**. Tall enough to **soak up** everything in the air, **carrying** the ball up the field and always finding **the right pass**.

On **two** separate occasions Ferdinand's transfers made him the **most expensive defender in the world**. There was a **very good reason** for that.

DOMINANCE **9**/10   DISTRIBUTION **9**/10   READING OF GAME **8**/10   YOUR RATING /10

CLUBS SUNDERLAND, LEEDS UNITED, ARSENAL, MANCHESTER CITY

COUNTRY ENGLAND

CAPS 117+ **PEAK** 2014-2019

HONOURS 3 ENGLISH LEAGUE TITLES, 4 FA CUPS, 5 LEAGUE CUPS

STEPH HOUGHTON

There's a **theme** running through all these **magnificent** players. So many started out **further up the pitch** and then dropped back, full of the **extra skills and vision** that would make them **stand out** in defence. Steph is the perfect example. Began as a **striker**, moved into **midfield**, now **bosses it all from the back** as captain of both Manchester City and England.

Tall, commanding, super-comfy on the ball. That's the **physical** side of it. Mentally, she is **nails**. Hard, pointy nails. **No one else has determination like her:** ignoring the PE teacher at school who told her she'd **never** be a professional footballer, coming back from a **broken leg** and a bad knee injury to **star** at successive World Cups.

Even now, with **over 100 England caps**, she is aiming to be the best player in the world. She says she **loves winning,** and that's the sort of attitude that **inspires** everyone around her. A team with Steph Houghton ruling the roost is a team that **scares** others. In the **nicest** possible way, of course.

DOMINANCE **9/10**   DISTRIBUTION **8/10**   READING OF GAME **8/10**   YOUR RATING **/10**

MANAGER'S NOTES

1. What does your team want more –
   a sweeper behind the defence like Baresi and
   Passarella, or a ball-player bringing it out like
   Moore and Scirea?

2. Bobby Moore lifted the World Cup for England.
   Mind you, Passarella did the same
   for Argentina...

3. (Style) counts in this position. Which player
   matches your own idea of cool?

THE DECISION

Who is going to be the second **centre-back** in your squad?
Draw them here, giving the trophy to your first choice,
and the medal to your second choice.
Don't forget to add their names to the silverware!

MASCOT

So. You've chosen your formation, the pre-match meal and your defence. Your team has a name, a badge, and – let's be honest – a **top** manager.

Now is the time to design your mascot, the furry creature who's going to be **dancing** round the pitch before games and **diving into the fans** when your team scores.

Four design tips to get the brain whirring:

Make them **alliterative** like Leicester's Filbert Fox. Even better if it **rhymes** like Man United's Fred the Red!

Use your **team's name or emblem** as the launchpad. See Watford's Harry the Hornet, Sheffield Wednesday's Ozzie the Owl or Southend's Sammy the Shrimp.

Bring back **extinct creatures**. There was nothing that connected Arsenal to dinosaurs. Until Gunnersaurus Rex, of course.

Look up **local legends**. Nottingham Forest knew what they were doing when they brought back Robin Hood in 2018. Bit harsh on Sherwood the Bear, but still …

My Mascot's Name:

What it looks like:

STADIUM

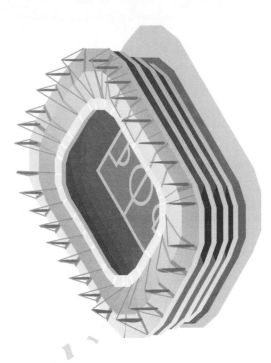

A great club must have a ground that fits its reputation and players. What will yours look like?

Work out the **capacity**, how many **tiers** the stands might have, whether it will be **one giant ring**, like Barca's Nou Camp, or **four distinct stands**, one down each side, like Liverpool's Anfield. Maybe one or more stands will be named after a **great player** of the past.

Maybe the **main home end** will have its own cool name – the Bank, the Kop, the Scoreboard End. Then there's the name for the **whole stadium**. You could take a load of cash off a company to call it after them, but that never sounds that special. 'The Hot and Spicy Peanuts Stadium'? **Horrible.** 'The Shiny Bot-Bot Toilet Bowl'? **Oh dear. Oh dear indeed.**

One thing that must be guaranteed: the pitch itself must be **perfect.** You've got the finest passers and ball-players of all time playing on it. Let's not give them a mud-bath.

Draw **your** dream stadium below.

Name: Date: Capacity:

Okay. This could be horrible or it could be beautiful.

Horrible because choosing just one from this list of absolute beauties is going to be impossibly hard. How you leave seven of them out is mind-frying. How you tell them is going to be a huge test of your management skills. 'Sit down, legend, I've got bad news for you ...'

Beautiful because you literally cannot go wrong. If you shut your eyes and just poked a finger at the page you'd still get one of the greatest players of all time. If you chew over all the evidence you're going to get someone who fans across the world love, like Fatty Foulke loves breakfasts.

So let's narrow this down. We've got options here in terms of style as well as impact. There are pure right wingers – the sort of dribbling heroes who appear to have the ball glued to the toes of their boots.

There are right midfielders, the sort who can place perfect crosses into the box and knock extraordinary cross-field passes about for fun, as well as working their bottoms off in defence as well as attack.

Then there are the forward men, the ones who start on the right but then go where they want, maybe cutting onto their left foot, maybe just generally rampaging.

It's a massive decision. Can you handle it?

CLUBS BOTAFOGO
COUNTRY BRAZIL
CAPS 50 **PEAK** 1958-1962
HONOURS 2 WORLD CUPS,
2 BRAZILIAN LEAGUE TITLES

GARRINCHA

Garrincha should **never** have been a footballer, if you went by **normal** standards. He dealt with that by blowing normal standards **out of the water.**

His right leg was six centimetres shorter than his left. It turned inwards as the left one went the other way. Garrincha dealt with that by turning defenders left and right and **inside out.** He was a **rascal** off the pitch. You're going to have to keep a close eye on him, otherwise he'll be off to the pub and **missing training.**

But when he **plays** for you, everything will make sense. The dribbling, the way he would **stop** with the ball and then **start again** and then **stop**, so the defender felt so **sea-sick** they wanted a lie-down. The **nutmegs.** Running off while leaving the ball behind and **laughing** as the defender ran with him rather than the ball.

Inside tip: Brazil **never lost a single game** when Pelé and Garrincha played together.

PACE **8/10**   TRICKS **10/10**   CROSSING **8/10**   **YOUR RATING** **/10**

CLUBS STOKE CITY, BLACKPOOL
COUNTRY ENGLAND
CAPS 54 **PEAK** 1950-1954
HONOURS FA CUP

STANLEY MATTHEWS

So many amazing Stan facts, so many reasons to pick him.

He played top-flight football until he was **50 years old**, in an era where most players were **cooked** at 32. He was so outstanding in inspiring Blackpool to come from 3–1 down against Bolton in the 1953 FA Cup final they called it the **Matthews Final** – which must have annoyed Blackpool's Stan Mortensen, who scored a **hat-trick!** He was the first man ever to **win the Ballon d'Or,** the annual award for the world's greatest player.

With Stan in your team you'll have a man who almost **invented** what a dribbling winger should be. He might just have been the **best crosser of the ball** in history.

He'll train relentlessly. Matthews ate loads of **fruit and veg** in an era when most players ate chips and smoked cigarettes. He also went running every morning in **lead boots,** so that when he came to matches in lighter boots he would be **so much fitter and faster.**

Oh – he was **never** booked. Not once. **Absolute diamond.**

PACE **6/10**   TRICKS **9/10**   CROSSING **10/10**   **YOUR RATING** /10

CLUBS MANCHESTER UNITED, LOS ANGELES AZTECS, FULHAM, FORT LAUDERDALE STRIKERS, HIBERNIAN, SAN JOSE EARTHQUAKES

COUNTRY NORTHERN IRELAND

CAPS 37 **PEAK** 1965-1969

HONOURS EUROPEAN CUP, 2 ENGLISH LEAGUE TITLES

GEORGE BEST

There's no two ways of saying this: **George could be a very naughty boy.** Parties. **Girlfriends. Drinking**. His favourite was parties where there would be both girlfriends **and** drinking. No manager **ever** tamed him. You'll have no harder task than keeping him on the straight and narrow. But it's **worth trying** because no one has ever been able to do what George could do on the pitch.

The most incredible dribbling. Impossible balance. So **cool** that he did everything before anyone else. He tried boots with **suckers** on the bottom rather than studs. He **kept going** even with defenders trying to kick him up in the air.

Everyone **loved** him. Maradona says he inspired him. He scored the critical goal as Manchester United won their first ever European Cup. He **should** have won so much more, but his wayward lifestyle got in the way. So few of his matches were televised, which means it's tough to find clips of him. But never has a player had a more suitable name. **Best. He was.**

PACE **9/10**	TRICKS **10/10**	CROSSING **9/10**	**YOUR RATING**	**/10**

CLUBS BOTAFOGO, MARSEILLE
COUNTRY BRAZIL
CAPS 81 **PEAK** 1968-1972
HONOURS WORLD CUP, COPA LIBERTADORES

JAIRZINHO

Garrincha blows everyone away. And then along comes a player for the **same club and country** who, in a very different way, keeps that streak of **brilliance** burning into the future. **Jairzinho was more direct.** He was stronger and scored more goals – in every single game, as Brazil **steamrollered** everyone in their path at the 1970 World Cup.

If he starts on the right for you, **be warned:** you'll be watching the game with a **massive grin** on your chops. **Skipping** past defenders, throwing little **bursts** of acceleration, hurdling challenges, **blasting** in shots and crosses. Jairzinho made it all look **fun.** Watch his goal against England in 1970. It's not just the finish, **thumping** though that was. It's the celebration afterwards. He can't stop jumping for joy. **Boing! Boing! Boing!**

That team had a **sensational** kit and played football to match. You could pick Jairzinho on the right, Carlos Alberto behind him at right-back and Pelé ahead of them both. **It's almost too good to be possible. But it is.**

PACE	9/10	TRICKS	8/10	CROSSING	9/10	YOUR RATING	/10

CLUBS MANCHESTER UNITED, REAL MADRID, LA GALAXY, A.C. MILAN, PARIS SAINT-GERMAIN

COUNTRY ENGLAND

CAPS 115

PEAK 1998-2002

HONOURS 2 FA CUPS, CHAMPIONS LEAGUE, 6 ENGLISH LEAGUE TITLES, SPANISH LEAGUE TITLE, FRENCH LEAGUE TITLE

DAVID BECKHAM

David Beckham is **so famous** that it's too easy to forget what a **remarkable** footballer he was. He wasn't fast. He didn't **need** to be. He only rarely dribbled past players. He didn't **have** to.

He didn't have to because **his right foot was capable of so much wonder.** His **passing** could take at least two defenders out of the game. His **crosses** could bend around a full-back and onto the **head** of his striker in the six-yard box. His **free-kicks** from outside the box could go top bins, bottom bins and **every bin in between.**

He ended up in the same **number 7 jersey** at United as George Best, but they were **very** different players. Becks got as good as he did by **practising** longer than anyone else. He stayed at the top for as long as he did by **never easing off.** At his best, maybe for England against Greece in 2002, he did **everything.**

Just don't let the **haircuts** and **fashion** get in the way. Becks was **special.**

| PACE | 6/10 | TRICKS | 7/10 | CROSSING | 10/10 | YOUR RATING | /10 |

CLUBS CHICAGO RED STARS, LYON, REIGN FC
COUNTRY USA
CAPS 160+ **PEAK** 2015-2019
HONOURS 2 WORLD CUPS, OLYMPIC GOLD, FRENCH LEAGUE TITLE, FRENCH CUP

MEGAN RAPINOE

Right-sided players don't **have** to bring you goals. A big part of their job is **bringing goals for team-mates** – crosses, little passes inside the full-backs, corners and whipped-in free-kicks. **Rapinoe can do all that.** She can **also** score at the rate of an out-and-out striker.

Twice in the last 16 and quarter-finals of the 2019 World Cup, **again** in the final against the Netherlands to win her the Golden Boot as the tournament's top scorer. Imagine if she'd scored **more than one** in the 13–0 group-stage demolition of Thailand. **Ouch.**

But the goals only make a **part** of the argument for choosing Rapinoe. She will **fight** for everyone in your team, no matter what their background, and has **campaigned** for female players to be paid the same as men – which is of course the policy of **this** team. She handles losses **brilliantly**, where other players might sulk and go into their shells. She will **lead from the front** and never take a backward step. And she will **celebrate** with total sincerity. No messing about. Arms out, **big grin. Have that, world . . .**

PACE **7/10**	TRICKS **8/10**	CROSSING **9/10**	YOUR RATING **/10**

CLUBS BARCELONA
COUNTRY ARGENTINA
CAPS 138+ **PEAK** 2012-2018
HONOURS 4 CHAMPIONS LEAGUES
10 SPANISH LEAGUE TITLES,
6 SPANISH CUPS

LIONEL MESSI

So, **right here** is our problem. You get your head around **how good** everyone is on this list, and then you come to Leo Messi and you just think, **what choice have I got?**

The balance, the pace, the dribbling. The impossible goals. The **non-stop** hard work, the **tricks,** the **acceleration** into spaces and gaps that no one else sees. Messi was meant to be **too small**. He turned into perhaps the **biggest** talent the game has ever seen. Maradona says he was his heir.

He can play up top, or just behind two strikers, or in a free role going **wherever he wants**. We've got him on the right so he can cut in onto his left foot and **wreak havoc** wherever he sees it.

You want **one goal to end all arguments?** Have a look at the solo wonder for Barca against Getafe. To have a player on your side who can do that is to be **blessed with unreal magic.**

| PACE 9/10 | TRICKS 10/10 | CROSSING 10/10 | YOUR RATING | /10 |

CLUBS AL MOKAWLOON, BASEL, CHELSEA, FIORENTINA, ROMA, LIVERPOOL
COUNTRY EGYPT
CAPS 67+ **PEAK** 2017-
HONOURS CHAMPIONS LEAGUE, 2 SWISS LEAGUE TITLES

MOHAMED SALAH

It's weird to even think it, but there was a time when managers **weren't picking** Salah. Mainly José Mourinho in one of his **grumpy** moods, but still. It's like having the **most amazing Formula 1 car** on your drive and only using it to pop out to **get some milk**.

Even now he's an unlikely hero. He doesn't show off. Sometimes he keeps a **straight face** when he scores. He gives loads of money to **charity**.

It works for him and for everyone watching. He notched **32 goals in 36 Premier League appearances** in his first season at Liverpool, the **critical** goal in the Champions League final in his second. He deserves a great **chant** from the Liverpool fans, so it's fitting he has **two.** They've seen the **wonder-goals,** they've seen the first touch, the step-overs, the cutting in and **bending** shots into the far corners.

You might start him on the right, but let him **push on as he likes**. Pick a central midfielder to **cover** behind him. **Formula 1 cars are designed to race.**

PACE **9/10**   TRICKS **9/10**   CROSSING **9/10**   YOUR RATING **/10**

MANAGER'S NOTES

1. What style of player works for your tactics – a dribbler like Stan, a midfielder who cuts in Messi-style, or a player who wants to attack like Rapinoe?

2. If you had to choose, would you prefer someone who mainly **creates** goals, like Becks, or someone who **scores** them like Salah?

3. There's some lively characters in here. Do you have the patience and management skills to bring out the best in them?

THE DECISION

Who is going to be the **right midfielder** in your squad?
Draw them here, giving the trophy to your first choice,
and the medal to your second choice.
Don't forget to add their names to the silverware!

The good news is that you've somehow managed to choose a right winger from an impossible list.
The bad news is that you've got the whole problem all over again on the left: finding a passer, a dribbler, a goalscorer and a setter-up of goals.

We can get through this. It's a good thing. Imagine if you were picking the worst team of all time, and had to choose a player from the eight worst lefties in history instead. Exactly.

Things to bear in mind as the manager of the Greatest Team Ever. You've all sorts of options here – wingers who will hug the touchline, mavericks who will start left but then make the most delightful runs into the box, workhorses who will run all day long, forward and back, to give your side support wherever it needs it.

You've also got a few more crazy cats. Divers. Party animals. They're going to bring the magic on the pitch but you'll have to get their heads right if they're going to produce their best for you.

It's a test of your managerial and coaching skills in every possible way. But when it's easy it's boring, right?

LEFT MIDFIELDERS / WINGERS

CLUBS DICK, KERR'S LADIES, PRESTON LADIES
COUNTRY ENGLAND
CAPS – **PEAK** 1922-1932

LILY PARR

Lily might be the **greatest player** too many people have **never heard of.**

Her **first season** playing proper football, and she scores **43 goals**. As a **14-year-old**. Jump on 30-odd years and she bags **900 goals** in her career in total, an outside-left rather than a left midfielder, so all about **attacking** the box and the byline and **smashing in shots** and crosses and then smashing in some more.

And smash is the right word. Lily was said to have the hardest shot in football. Imagine having a player with a shot so powerful that one of her penalties **broke the arm** of the goalkeeper daft enough to get in the way. **Youch.**

On the **downside**, Lily was a **smoker.** She would even have a cigarette on the **touchline** before games. You're going to have to **sort that out.** They're good for no one.

On the **upside**, she was tall, strong and **incredibly brave**. Superb left-foot crosses, lofted cross-field passes from one wing to the other.

| PACE | 8/10 | TRICKS | 8/10 | CROSSING | 9/10 | YOUR RATING | /10 |

CLUBS PRESTON NORTH END
COUNTRY ENGLAND
CAPS 76 **PEAK** 1953-1958

TOM FINNEY

Ignore the lack of big-time honours. Take heed instead of what these **wise men** said about Sir Tom.

Bill Shankly, legendary Liverpool manager: **'Finney was the greatest I ever saw.'**
Tommy Docherty, former Man United manager: **'Messi is Finney reborn.'**

Bobby Charlton was **so awestruck** when he got to play with Finney for England that he could barely believe it was happening. Finney then **pinged in** a peach of a cross for Bobby's **first international goal.** Classic Tom touch.

You could play Tom **on the right or up front** and he'll still be the **best player** on the pitch. He wasn't **big.** He's not going to demand **big wages** either – he was a plumber who carried on plumbing even after all those England goals. They called his Preston team **the plumber and 10 drips,** which was a bit harsh. But possibly fair.

He was also maybe the **nicest** man ever to play for England. Okay, joint nicest with Jimmy Armfield. **No whinging or diving or moaning** from those two. Only the good stuff.

PACE **9/10**	TRICKS **7/10**	CROSSING **9/10**	**YOUR RATING** **/10**

CLUBS MANCHESTER UNITED
COUNTRY WALES
CAPS 64   **PEAK** 1994-1999
HONOURS 2 CHAMPIONS LEAGUES,
13 ENGLISH LEAGUE TITLES, 4 FA CUPS,
3 LEAGUE CUPS

RYAN GIGGS

Some might say that **the only question with Giggsy is which era Giggsy you pick.**

The **teenager** who dribbled like George Best. The **20-something** who won the Champions League and scored, against Arsenal, maybe the **greatest goal in FA Cup history.** The **30-something** who pushed inside off his wing and ran the game from there instead.

You can't go wrong with any of them. Here's a fact to blow the mind: Giggs individually has **won more league titles than every club in England except Man United and Liverpool.** One player. All those clubs. That's **how good** he was, for how long.

His football **brain** was as fast as his legs; he'll spot passes for you then find the **perfect weight** to make them reality. No-one in the history of the Premier League has **set up more goals.**

Need more evidence? Search online for his goals. There's a reason his chant at Old Trafford went the way it did. "**Giggs! Giggs will tear you apart, again.**"

PACE **9/10**	TRICKS **9/10**	CROSSING **9/10**	YOUR RATING **/10**

CLUBS TYRESÖ FF, WASHINGTON WARTHOGS, DELAWARE GENIES, BOSTON BREAKERS, KIF ÖREBRO DFF

COUNTRY USA

CAPS 354 **PEAK** 1995-2000

HONOURS WORLD CUP, 2 OLYMPIC GOLDS

KRISTINE LILLY

Hang on a second. Let's just look at that number of caps again. **How many? HOW MANY?**

David Beckham is considered a hero for playing **115 times** for his country. Which spells out quite how remarkable a player Lilly was to make three times as many international appearances. **No player in the history of the game has won more caps. Fact.**

Very few players have brought her **all-round game** to the left side of midfield. And she was a complete midfielder too – **a goal more than once every three games** for the US, scorer of a **critical penalty** in the 1999 World Cup final shoot-out, masterful with left-footed free-kicks, delicate chips and blasting drives from distance.

But she would **work back** as well as charge on. That final in '99 only went to penalties because Lilly pulled off a brilliant headed **goal-line clearance** with the game at 0-0

She played in **five World Cups.** Her managers knew. Now **you** do too.

| PACE **7/10** | TRICKS **7/10** | CROSSING **9/10** | YOUR RATING **/10** |

CLUBS SOUTHAMPTON, TOTTENHAM HOTSPUR, REAL MADRID

COUNTRY WALES

CAPS 82+ **PEAK** 2010-2015

HONOURS 4 CHAMPIONS LEAGUES, SPANISH LEAGUE TITLE, SPANISH CUP

GARETH BALE

So we know what Bale can do. We've seen the **outrageous pace.** We've seen the **volleys,** the **overhead** kicks.

We've seen the **crosses** placed **precisely** onto the head or foot of onrushing team-mates. We're familiar with the **free-kicks** spanked home from **miles** out. There's the goal v Barca in 2014 when he actually **runs off the pitch** to get round his man. Yes, Gareth Bale is **so quick** he can run away from goal and still end up getting there before anyone else.

That's not the challenge for you as a manager. **It's getting him on the pitch.** It's getting him on the pitch with his **head** right. No more **niggling injuries.** No more starring in **fits and starts.**

Find the **true** Bale and let him **drive** your team on like he drove Wales to the semis of the 2016 European Championships and Madrid to all those Champions League wins.

Find him, and **free** him.

| PACE | **10/10** | TRICKS | **7/10** | CROSSING | **9/10** | YOUR RATING | **/10** |

CLUBS SPORTING LISBON. MANCHESTER UNITED, REAL MADRID, JUVENTUS

COUNTRY PORTUGAL

CAPS 164+ **PEAK** 2006-2014

HONOURS EUROPEAN CHAMPIONSHIP, 5 CHAMPIONS LEAGUES, 3 ENGLISH LEAGUE TITLES, FA CUP, 2 LEAGUE CUPS, 2 SPANISH LEAGUE TITLES, 2 SPANISH CUPS, ITALIAN LEAGUE TITLE

CRISTIANO RONALDO

What. A. Player. Okay, he can be a bit of a **poser.** He wears swimming trunks on holiday that **no-one else** could even consider, let alone sport on the beach. But that's all the negative. The rest is so **beautifully positive** it could make you dance about the room with happiness.

The pace, the trickery. The step-overs, the **Ronaldo Chop.** The knuckleball free-kicks, when he hits through the **valve** of the ball to make it **dip and swerve** and leave goalkeepers on their backsides. The astonishing ability to seemingly **hang** in the air before powering a header into the goal. He could play **anywhere** across the front of this team. He could play centre-mid. Start him on the left and let him go like a **crazy firework.**

Let's lob in a few **juicy stats.** Real Madrid's **all-time top goal-scorer.** 34 hat-tricks in the Spanish league, eight in one season alone. The **only man in history** to score 30 or more goals in **six** consecutive La Liga campaigns. **Even Messi couldn't do that.** Your team could be the first ever to feature both Ronaldo **and** Messi. **Together. At last. Gulp.**

| PACE 9/10 | TRICKS 10/10 | CROSSING 9/10 | YOUR RATING /10 |

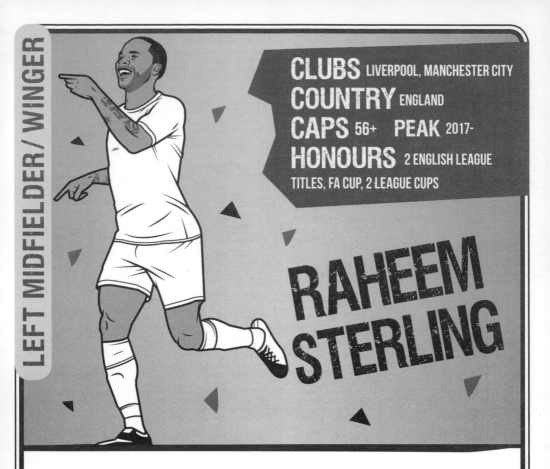

CLUBS LIVERPOOL, MANCHESTER CITY
COUNTRY ENGLAND
CAPS 56+ **PEAK** 2017-
HONOURS 2 ENGLISH LEAGUE TITLES, FA CUP, 2 LEAGUE CUPS

RAHEEM STERLING

You can hear **the chat** now. Sterling's scored goals, **but others have scored more.** What if he stops improving?

But here's the thing. He **hasn't** stopped improving yet. He started **great** and gets **better** with every season.

There was always the **pace.** Then came a ruthlessness to his **finishing.** No more stumbles. Suddenly his one-on-ones **always** find the back of the net.

Now it's the **movement.** Seeing where the chance might come, **timing his run** to beat the defence and offside trap to arrive at the **magic** moment.

It'll be something else next. And that's why Sterling is worth your shout. Pick him and you get his present but also his **future.** He can play left, he can play up front, he can play in between. His future is **so bright** we might all have to wear sunglasses.

PACE **10/10**   TRICKS **8/10**   CROSSING **8/10**   **YOUR RATING** **/10**

CLUBS SANTOS, BARCELONA, PARIS SAINT-GERMAIN

COUNTRY BRAZIL

CAPS 101+ **PEAK** 2015-

HONOURS OLYMPIC GOLD, CHAMPIONS LEAGUE, COPA LIBERTADORES, 2 SPANISH LEAGUE TITLES, 3 SPANISH CUPS, 2 FRENCH LEAGUE TITLES, FRENCH CUP, BRAZILIAN CUP

NEYMAR

Neymar can do everything. But a lot of people would say he dives. He can **dribble** like Maradona. But he dives. He's got **tricks** like Ronaldo. But he dives. He can **link up** in your team with Messi and Andrés Iniesta and Dani Alves like he did for Barcelona. **But he dives.**

And so it comes down to **two questions** for you, his new manager.

1. Can you **change** the habit of a lifetime and get him to **stay on his feet?**

2. If you can't, does his **outrageous talent** make him **worth it** anyway?

So many goals for Brazil. He might well overtake **Pelé's** total one day. Such **balance** – you can tell that he loves to dance, because when he's stepping through a defence it's like he's listening to **music** that no-one else can hear. All those **fakes,** making defenders stop or step the wrong way, all those **brakes,** when he comes to a dead halt and then accelerates away again while his opponent is still trying to slow down. Goals, assists, **pure entertainment.** But he dives. **Your team. Your call.**

| PACE 9/10 | TRICKS 10/10 | CROSSING 8/10 | YOUR RATING /10 |

MANAGER'S NOTES

1. You could have **Messi** and **Ronaldo** in the same team. Deep breaths. (Messi and Ronaldo) in the **same** team!

2. You want a team who knows how to **win?** Look at the number of **titles** bagged by Giggsy or the **World Cup** campaigns of Kristine Lilly ...

3. The best teams **get on** with each other, and no-one ever fell out with Tom Finney. Equally, no-one can **keep up** with Bale or Sterling ...

THE DECISION

Who is going to be the **left midfielder** in your squad?
Draw them here, giving the trophy to your first choice,
and the medal to your second choice.
Don't forget to add their names to the silverware!

KIT

You're not a team without a **sweet kit to wear,** a shirt that makes you **stand out** from the rest, a look that **everyone** takes one look at and instantly thinks – **ooh yeah,** I fancy one of those . . .

A couple of **pointers before you** draw your design:

COLOUR

Look in your wardrobe, work out what works for you, run with it. Still unsure? Lots of famous clubs based their original designs on the colours of the school that provided the majority of its early players and staff. Others were based on kits that were borrowed – for example, Juventus' famous black-and-white stripes came from being given a set of Notts County shirts as they started out.

PATTERN

Plain or stripes? If stripes, horizontal ones or hoops? Broad, even ones or pinstripes?

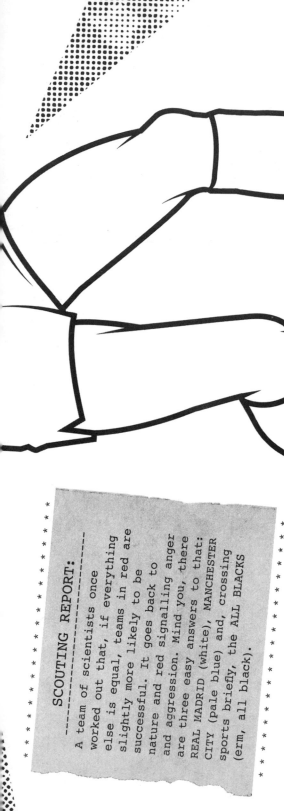

SPONSOR

A great sponsor's name sets the rest of the kit off a treat. You could choose a business that's local to you. Maybe it's your favourite thing in the world – a sportswear brand, a gaming console. Maybe you'll do a Barca 2006–12 and put a charity on the front. Let's face it, you've already got the greatest players in history. It's not like you need more money to buy anyone else …

CONTRAST

Shorts the same colour as the shirt, or something that complements the shirt? Liverpool go red all the way, City pair the blue shirt with white shorts. England's home kit combines white shirt with blue shorts.

BOOTS

Your superstars will like to look good. They'll want the perfect footwear to match their perfect touch.

Sketch out your own patented **luxury football boots** here – complete with logo, name, colour and choice of sole.

Decisions, decision, decisions.

This team is coming together a treat. Already you pity the side that's going to walk out of the tunnel and see this line-up waiting to take them on.

Now for a critical piece of the jigsaw. You can get everything right at the back and on the wings, but if that opposition can cut through you every time, none of it will matter. It's like trying to run without a spine. Impossible.

We'll get to our attacking midfielders in a few pages. For now it's about the one who makes it all tick alongside them, the engine in our car. Tackle, pass, run. Again and again and again.

All manner of options here. You could go pure defensive midfielder, ruining the opposition's day, nicking the ball time and again, breaking their hearts and minds. You could go box-to-box ball of energy, running the show down the middle. You could go deep playmaker, spraying the ball around, conducting the orchestra like a true artist.

Decisions, decisions. All of them good ones.

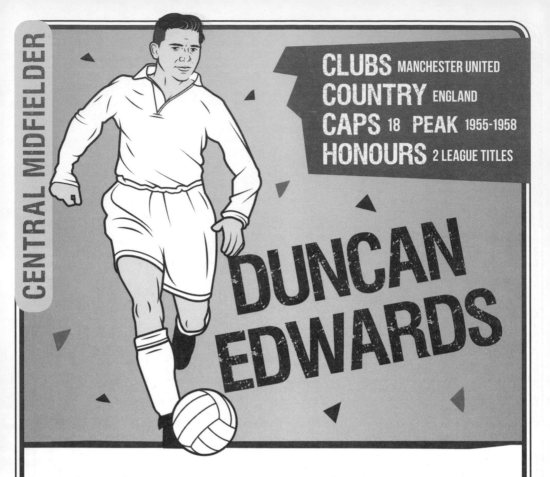

CLUBS MANCHESTER UNITED
COUNTRY ENGLAND
CAPS 18 **PEAK** 1955-1958
HONOURS 2 LEAGUE TITLES

DUNCAN EDWARDS

So much **wonder** in Edwards' game, so much **tragedy** in the way it was **cut short**.

Edwards was only 21 years old when he was killed, along with **seven** other Manchester United players, in the Munich air disaster of 1958. He had already done **so much** for United and England that people understood his **greatness** and what he could have gone on to do.

He was big. He was strong. He could sit in front of the defence and run all day, but it was the **creative stuff** he did with the ball that set him apart – the **range** of his passing, the way he would come **steaming forward** with the ball, the **power** in the shots he would unleash. Had Edwards lived, people say he would have developed into the **finest player in the world.**

United and England **mourned** him for years. To have even **one** more game from Duncan might be the **greatest wonder** of all.

TACKLING **9/10**   PASSING **9/10**   ENERGY **9/10**   **YOUR RATING** /10

CLUBS MADUREIRA, FLUMINENSE, BOTAFOGO, REAL MADRID, CD VERACRUZ

COUNTRY BRAZIL

CAPS 68 **PEAK** 1958-1962

HONOURS 2 WORLD CUPS, EUROPEAN CUP

DIDI

So much to **love** about Didi, so much he's going to bring to your team. He could **tackle.** He could **pass.** He could **curl in free-kicks** and he could unleash hell with **blasters** from **miles** out.

He even invented a new sort of **late-dipping**, **late-swerving** free-kick called the **Dry Leaf** (because of the way a leaf swerves in the wind). Ronaldo before Ronaldo. 12 of his 20 international goals came from **dead-ball situations,** and this in a team that included free-kick **superheroes** Pelé and Garrincha.

He was voted the **best player** at the 1958 World Cup, the first that Brazil ever won. He repeatedly set up Pelé at the 1962 World Cup. All the while so **calm** under pressure, so composed on the ball. All the time **working** so hard, because he had grown up so poor, **selling peanuts on the street as a kid** to make ends meet. Everyone loved him. **The original midfield general**.

| TACKLING | 8/10 | PASSING | 8/10 | ENERGY | 8/10 | YOUR RATING | /10 |

CLUBS AJAX, A.C. MILAN
COUNTRY THE NETHERLANDS
CAPS 73 **PEAK** 1988-1992
HONOURS EUROPEAN CHAMPIONSHIP, 3 EUROPEAN CUPS/CHAMPIONS LEAGUES, EUROPEAN CUP-WINNER'S CUP, 5 DUTCH LEAGUE TITLES, 3 DUTCH CUPS, 2 ITALIAN LEAGUE TITLES

FRANK RIJKAARD

Rijkaard once did the thing to another footballer that all players **hate** more than anything else in the game. **World Cup, 1990. The Netherlands vs Germany.** German striker Rudi Voller **annoying** Rijkaard, fouling him all the time. Frank holds his temper, holds his temper . . . **and then spits in Rudi's hair.** Twice. **Not nice.**

But don't let that put you off. It was out of character, because that character was a defensive midfielder who inspired one of the all-time great European club sides and **held together** a brilliant if stroppy Dutch team.

He's 6ft 3in (1.9m), so he's winning **all the headers and 50/50s** for you. To be fair, he's **probably** winning the 40/60s and the 30/70s as well. Able to read the game **so accurately** it's like he's watched it already on some weird **future-world** streaming service. **Elegant** on the ball, **super** long-range passing.

One more shout: he played brilliantly with finisher-supreme Marco van Basten. But he had **rows** with Johan Cruyff, so maybe leave those two apart.

| TACKLING | 8/10 | PASSING | 9/10 | ENERGY | 8/10 | YOUR RATING | /10 |

CLUBS TYRESÖ FF, ORLANDO LIONS WOMEN
COUNTRY USA
CAPS 153 **PEAK** 1991-1996
HONOURS 2 WORLD CUPS, OLYMPIC GOLD

MICHELLE AKERS

Great players make their mark on great occasions. They find a **little something extra**. They don't wait for **someone else** to seize the moment. They grab it themselves and **refuse** to let go.

It's the 1991 World Cup final, the **first** in women's football history, Norway up against the USA, Pelé the guest of honour in the 60,000-strong crowd. **Everyone is nervous**. The game is **tighter** than a tutu on a hippo. **Bang.** Michelle Akers runs on to a deep cross and **buries** a header into the far corner: 1–0. Norway equalise. With **two minutes** to go, the final is drifting towards extra time. The ball is bouncing around the Norwegian back four. **Akers pounces.** One touch **past** the defender, into the box, **round** the keeper, **cheeky tap** with the left foot, right foot **stroking it home**.

That's Michelle Akers in one match. That's why she was named FIFA's **Female Player of the Century** jointly with China's Sun Wen. Strong, physically dominant, determined to fight for **everything**. You cannot ask for more than Akers brings.

TACKLING	8/10	PASSING	9/10	ENERGY	10/10	YOUR RATING	/10

CLUBS MANCHESTER UNITED
COUNTRY ENGLAND
CAPS 66 **PEAK** 1999-2004
HONOURS 2 CHAMPIONS LEAGUES, 11 ENGLISH LEAGUE TITLES, 3 FA CUPS, 2 LEAGUE CUPS

PAUL SCHOLES

Here's an **almost impossible** question about an **almost impossibly good** player: if Paul Scholes looked like David Beckham and Beckham looked like Scholes, **who would be more famous?** Scholes didn't care about **flashy** cars or big boot-deals. He didn't have tattoos or his **own range of aftershave.** It was all about **football.** Always.

Zidane described him as his **toughest** opponent, the **complete** midfielder. Pep Guardiola said he was the best midfielder of his generation. Pelé kept it simple: 'If he was playing with me, I would have scored more goals.' **Pelé scored 1,281 goals. Exactly.**

It wasn't about **pace** or dribbling with Scholes. It was his **passing**, his **movement** into the box, the way he could **strike a ball on the volley** or put it **anywhere** he wanted.

You might have to work on his **tackling,** or get someone else to do it for him. Only Sergio Ramos has received more yellow cards in the Champions League. You'll need to work on **nothing else.** Apart from your **thanks,** when he wins game after game for you.

| TACKLING | 8/10 | PASSING | 10/10 | ENERGY | 8/10 | YOUR RATING | /10 |

CLUBS LIVERPOOL, LA GALAXY
COUNTRY ENGLAND
CAPS 114
PEAK 2004-2009
HONOURS CHAMPIONS LEAGUE, UEFA CUP, 2 FA CUPS, 3 LEAGUE CUPS

STEVEN GERRARD

Stick down a **wish-list** of **everything** you'd want from your centre midfielder. Tackling. Stamina. Leadership. Goals, passing, free-kicks. You could keep adding **as many attributes** as you liked. Steven Gerrard **would have them all,** because he was the **perfect** modern midfielder.

Gerrard was **so good** that you could play him on the right wing, or behind the front two, or **even** at right-back, and he'd **still** be the best player on the pitch and he'd still be **running the game**.

Not **all** superstar players love the game. Some do it just for the **money**. Some do it only in the matches they think matter **most**. Gerrard did it **every day in training** and **every time** he pulled on the shirt of Liverpool or England. He will **set the standard** for you and **drag** every other player up to it. Zinedine Zidane said in 2009 that Gerrard was better that year than Messi and Ronaldo. **No one** argued.

| TACKLING | 9/10 | PASSING | 9/10 | ENERGY | 10/10 | YOUR RATING | /10 |

CLUBS BEVEREN, METALURH DONETSK, OLYMPIACOS, MONACO, BARCELONA, MANCHESTER CITY

COUNTRY IVORY COAST

CAPS 101 **PEAK** 2009-2015

HONOURS AFRICA CUP OF NATIONS, CHAMPIONS LEAGUE, 3 ENGLISH LEAGUE TITLES, FA CUP, 2 LEAGUE CUPS, 2 SPANISH LEAGUE TITLES, SPANISH CUP

YAYA TOURÉ

Proper test of your man-management skills, this. There was a moment during Yaya's trophy-drenched spell at Manchester City when it looked like he was going to **leave** without any warning. The issue wasn't **money**, or **injury**, or a **row** with the manager. It was about his **birthday.**

City had given him a **cake.** His agent wanted **more.** Handshakes from the owners. Maybe, he **hinted**, the same birthday present that Roberto Carlos had got from his club: an **£800,000 Bugatti Veyron.** Yaya blamed the agent. City **forgave** him. He was so powerful through the middle, so **non-stop** in his running, so sweet with his shooting, that you could **never** be angry with him for long.

Play him defensive and he **owns** your half for you. Let him go box-to-box and he'll **rampage like some beautiful runaway train.** Need any more convincing? His goals were **stunners.** There's a reason he was four times voted African Footballer of the Year. His birthday, by the way, is 13 May. **Just in case, yeah?**

| TACKLING | 8/10 | PASSING | 9/10 | ENERGY | 10/10 | YOUR RATING | /10 |

CLUBS BOULOGNE, CAEN, LEICESTER CITY, CHELSEA

COUNTRY FRANCE

CAPS 39+ **PEAK** 2015-2018

HONOURS WORLD CUP, EUROPA LEAGUE, 2 ENGLISH LEAGUE TITLES, FA CUP

N'GOLO KANTÉ

You want a **pure defensive midfielder?** Job done. **Look no further.**

Seems **ludicrous**, looking back, but there **was** a time when big clubs didn't **bother** with Kanté because they thought he was too **small.** Then came his season with Leicester, when he made **31 more tackles** than any other player in the Premier League as the Foxes pulled off a glorious shock title win. Oh – and **15 more interceptions** than anyone else either.

Tackles. Interceptions. That's **all** you need to know about Kanté. It's why he **won** the Premier League with Chelsea the following season, and the World Cup with France the year after that too. Such energy. Such **positioning**. Always **breaking up play,** always finding the **right** little pass to a team-mate.

As a **youngster** at Boulogne, Kanté used a **scooter** to get to training – not a **motorised** one, just one where you **push** and glide. That's not **normal** for a footballer. But neither is 175 tackles and 157 interceptions in one Premier League season. Others can't. **Kanté can.**

TACKLING	10/10	PASSING	7/10	ENERGY	10/10	YOUR RATING	/10

MANAGER'S NOTES

1. What works best for your style: defensive <u>shield</u> like Kanté and Rijkaard or a box-to-boxer like Gerrard and Touré?

2. You need (goals?) Then do you need Scholes?

3. How much 'height' is there in the rest of your team? Do you need more here or are you covered elsewhere?

THE DECISION

Who is going to be the **central midfielder** in your squad?
Draw them here, giving the trophy to your first choice,
and the medal to your second choice.
Don't forget to add their names to the silverware!

No two ways about it, there's a spark of beautiful madness about many of these players. Maybe it goes with the role. All that creativity and brilliance leaks out in other ways, good and bad.

Attacking midfielders want to out-fun everyone instead. Crazy dribbling, genius ball control. Ridiculous goals, from close in after skipping past falling-over defenders, from outside the box having decided to take them out of the game by shooting before they can get close.

Passes that no one else sees, that no one else could make. There's another thread that ties them together too: they all bring magic to the football pitch. You watch them and you can't help but smile, or whoop, or stand up and roar your head off with delight.

That's what attacking midfielders do. There's no pleasure for them in stopping other teams having fun. Tackling is left to others. Defending on corners is not their strong suit.

It's why a lot of people would love to be one. And why choosing the best for your team is going to be pure pleasure.

CLUBS VENEZIA, TORINO
COUNTRY ITALY
CAPS 12 **PEAK** 1941-1946
HONOURS 5 ITALIAN LEAGUE TITLES, 2 ITALIAN CUPS

VALENTINO MAZZOLA

Sometimes a player comes along who changes how everyone thinks about the game. It sort of freaks people out. 'Hey. How come **you're** doing stuff that it used to require **three** people to do?'

That's Mazzola. He's a scorer of **lots** of goals and he's a scorer of **great** goals. He creates heaps of them for **others**. He's strong in the air, and he can beat players **on the run** like their feet are glued to the ground with **Super-Stick No-Move Glue-Shoes.**

The **fastest hat-trick** in Italian league history – **three goals in two minutes**. A man **so good** at dribbling that in certain parts of Italy the word for dribblers is **'veneziani'**, based on Mazzola's first club Venezia, because people had never seen anything like it before.

He should be easy to manage. To relax he didn't go out partying or drive flash cars but **played bowls**. Hmm. Ideal for keeping him **fresh** for your big games. Just maybe don't put him in charge of organising the club **Christmas party. Yawn.**

PASSING **8/10**   VISION **8/10**   STYLE **8/10**   **YOUR RATING** **/10**

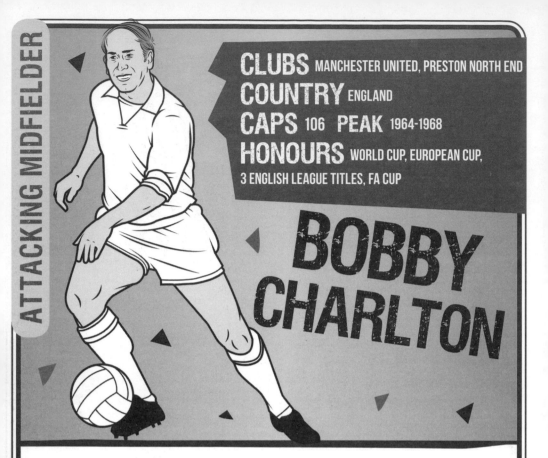

CLUBS MANCHESTER UNITED, PRESTON NORTH END
COUNTRY ENGLAND
CAPS 106 **PEAK** 1964-1968
HONOURS WORLD CUP, EUROPEAN CUP, 3 ENGLISH LEAGUE TITLES, FA CUP

BOBBY CHARLTON

Of **all** the stirring sights that football has produced, there is **nothing more joyous** than Bobby Charlton **storming forward** and launching into a **long-range cannonball shot.**

Defenders **stumbling** in his wake. Bobby in **mid-air**, right foot pointing out in front of him, left foot tucked behind. The ball **screaming** into the top corner like it's been **fired from a catapult,** the goalkeeper throwing himself **pointlessly** in its slipstream. Bobby was all about **attacking.** The runs, the passes, the shooting. He was the **heartbeat** of the first Man United team to win the European Cup, and he would be the heartbeat of **yours** too.

Charlton in one moment? Watch the clip of his goal for England against Mexico at Wembley in 1966. Look at the **'keeper's reaction** afterwards. It's **destroyed** him. He can't actually **move**. Two goals as United captain in that 1968 European Cup final, finishing his career with England as **record goal-scorer** and with a **record number of caps.** A wonderful man who will give you everything he has.

PASSING	9/10	VISION	9/10	STYLE	9/10	YOUR RATING	/10

CLUBS NANCY, SAINT-ÉTIENNE, JUVENTUS
COUNTRY FRANCE
CAPS 72 **PEAK** 1982-1986
HONOURS EUROPEAN CHAMPIONSHIP, EUROPEAN CUP, EUROPEAN CUP-WINNERS' CUP, 2 ITALIAN LEAGUE TITLES, ITALIAN CUP, FRENCH LEAGUE TITLE, FRENCH CUP

MICHEL PLATINI

If Michel Platini comes up to you in training and says he wants to do **less hard running**, don't worry about it. If he's not getting **stuck in** to tackling drills, **cut him some slack.** Platini **isn't like other players** and you're going to have to manage him **differently.**

You will have **stronger** players and you will have **faster** players. What you might not have is someone with his **massive football brain.** If you were to **flip up** the top of his head and look inside, you'd probably see **loads** of little footballs.

Platini saw **chances** where other players saw **defenders**. Three times winner of the Ballon d'Or, three times top scorer in the Italian league, as a **midfielder**. Top scorer when France won the 1984 European Championship with **nine** goals, out of his team's total of 14, in just **five** games. They called him **Le Roi,** The King, for a very good reason.

Oh – he also wore two of the **coolest kits of all time**. Juve '83, France '84. **Legend.**

PASSING	9/10	VISION	10/10	STYLE	10/10	YOUR RATING	/10

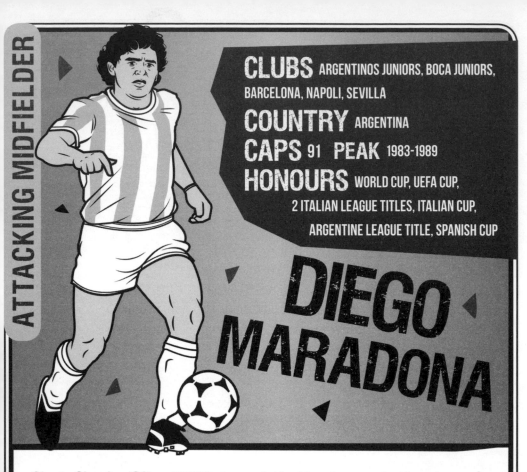

CLUBS ARGENTINOS JUNIORS, BOCA JUNIORS, BARCELONA, NAPOLI, SEVILLA

COUNTRY ARGENTINA

CAPS 91 **PEAK** 1983-1989

HONOURS WORLD CUP, UEFA CUP, 2 ITALIAN LEAGUE TITLES, ITALIAN CUP, ARGENTINE LEAGUE TITLE, SPANISH CUP

DIEGO MARADONA

Short. Chunky. Often angry. A nasty habit of hanging around with **nasty people.** Maradona should have been a **failure.** Instead he might be the **greatest** footballer who ever lived. A **dribbler** like none before. A **force** who would drag his teams to fresh triumphs. A scorer of goals that mattered and goals **you could never forget.**

And everyone knows it. The things I could do with a **football,** said Platini, Maradona could do with an **orange. No** way of stopping him, said Franco Baresi.

Oh, he could be **cruel.** The **handball** goal against England at the '86 World Cup. But then there's his **second** goal against England, maybe the **greatest** ever scored. Past **five** opponents, past Peter Shilton in goal. **Unstoppable, impossible, unbeatable.**

How **amazing** would he be for you? Let the Argentine commentary for that goal spell it out. **'Goaaal! I want to cry!** Holy God, **long live football!** Oh, what a goal! Diegoal! Maradona! The greatest play of all time – **what planet did you come from?'**

| PASSING | **10/10** | VISION | **10/10** | STYLE | **9/10** | YOUR RATING | **/10** |

CLUBS NEWCASTLE UNITED, TOTTENHAM HOTSPUR, LAZIO, RANGERS, MIDDLESBROUGH, EVERTON, BURNLEY
COUNTRY ENGLAND
CAPS 57 **PEAK** 1988-1991
HONOURS FA CUP, 2 SCOTTISH LEAGUE TITLES, SCOTTISH CUP, SCOTTISH LEAGUE CUP

PAUL GASCOIGNE

Let's be **honest** here: **Gazza could be a maverick.** He was once booked for showing a humourless ref the **yellow card he'd just retrieved for him!** He could be a **good** maverick, playing loads of **practical jokes** on his team-mates, training **harder and longer** than anyone else, bringing all that crazy **energy** to the pitch and using it to blow rival teams apart. Or he could be a **bad** maverick, staying out **too late**, eating too much **bad food, drinking** too much bad drink. To capture the **best** of him you'll have to keep the **worst** of him at bay.

It's **worth** your time and energy because **Good Gazza** had **so** much talent he could win matches **on his own** for you. Pinging **genius passes** all over the place. Crashing in free-kicks. Dribbling and barging his way past defenders with **proper upper-body strength.** He's an **unstoppable ball** of legs and elbows and **energy**.

And he loves it. He **loves** football, and he **loves** using his gifts to make other people love football **even more**.

| PASSING | 10/10 | VISION | 9/10 | STYLE | 8/10 | YOUR RATING | /10 |

CLUBS CANNES, BORDEAUX, JUVENTUS, REAL MADRID

COUNTRY FRANCE

CAPS 108 **PEAK** 1998-2002

HONOURS WORLD CUP, EUROPEAN CHAMPIONSHIP, CHAMPIONS LEAGUE, 2 ITALIAN LEAGUE TITLES, SPANISH LEAGUE TITLE

ZINEDINE ZIDANE

Maradona wore the number 10 shirt and defined it; Zidane **inherited** it. Zidane could **hold on to the ball** as if he had an enchanted force-field around him. **Little flicks, turns, tricks** to leave defenders staring the **wrong way** and wondering where on earth he'd gone.

His **goal** for Real Madrid in the final of the 2002 Champions League, with his **weaker left foot**, is a volley so **perfect** it looks like it came from a **FIFA 20 hack**. David Beckham and Roberto Carlos, who played with him during his time at Madrid, reckoned he was the greatest of all time. As recommendations go, it's a **mighty** powerful one.

Like Maradona, he had a temper. He was shown **14 red cards** in his career, and was sent off in both the group stage of the 1998 World Cup **and** the final in 2006 (possibly costing France the trophy).

But he could be the **magic dust** your team needs. Not least if you pick him with Thierry Henry up front. The **creator** and the **finisher**, together once again.

| PASSING | **9/10** | VISION | **9/10** | STYLE | **9/10** | YOUR RATING | /10 |

CLUBS GRÊMIO, PARIS SAINT-GERMAIN, BARCELONA, A.C. MILAN, FLAMENGO, ATLÉTICO MINEIRO, QUERÉTARO, FLUMINENSE

COUNTRY BRAZIL

CAPS 97 **PEAK** 2002-2006

HONOURS WORLD CUP, COPA AMÉRICA, COPA LIBERTADORES, CHAMPIONS LEAGUE, 2 SPANISH LEAGUE TITLES, ITALIAN LEAGUE TITLE

RONALDINHO

Warning: if you make space for this **dancing** Brazilian prodigy in your side, be prepared to make space for a **helicopter** at the training ground. That's how he liked to **get around**. That's how he could get to **so many parties** and still just about get back in time for training.

You might also need to make space for **dizzy defenders** to have a good lie-down. Ronaldinho kills with his **skills.** It's why he was **twice** FIFA World Player of the Year. At his best the rest couldn't get **close**.

His **balance** was incredible. Skipping through midfields, breaking out his **classic elastico move**, where his foot would start pushing the ball **one way** only to suddenly snap back and flick it **the other.** All done at **extreme pace**, all done at extreme pace, as impossible to stop as a summer storm. Search out his display against England at the 2002 World Cup. **Stepover City** to set up Brazil's equaliser, **cheekiness** and skill to bend in the winner.

Give him the ball. Watch him go.

| PASSING | 8/10 | VISION | 9/10 | STYLE | 9/10 | YOUR RATING | /10 |

CLUBS BARCELONA, VISSEL KOBE
COUNTRY SPAIN
CAPS 131 **PEAK** 2008-2012
HONOURS WORLD CUP,
2 EUROPEAN CHAMPIONSHIPS, 4 CHAMPIONS
LEAGUES, 9 SPANISH LEAGUE TITLES,
6 SPANISH CUPS

ANDRÉS INIESTA

You don't need to be big to **boss** the biggest games. **You don't need to be flashy** to be the **brightest light** on the pitch.

No Spanish player in history has won more than Iniesta's **35 trophies**. Always in the **right place**, always putting his pass to a **better place still**. Playing with his **head up**, calculating the **angles**, making everything work.

They called him **The Brain** and they **knew** what they were doing. Iniesta will be **inspired** in your team because he inspires **all** those around him. Man of the match as Spain won their **first ever** World Cup in 2010, scorer of the **winning** goal with the game locked in extra time.

If you want tricks he's got **La Croqueta**, which involves a **drag** with one foot and **flick** to the other. If you want a **pure playmaker**, rather than a relentless scorer, Iniesta is the one for you. Zinedine Zidane, not known for his modesty, once said of Iniesta, **'He reminds me of myself.'** High praise **indeed.**

| PASSING | 9/10 | VISION | 9/10 | STYLE | 8/10 | YOUR RATING | /10 |

MANAGER'S NOTES

1. So many of these superstars bring trouble as well as genius – have you got the time and energy as a manager to handle them?

2. If you pick Gazza, he'll play jokes on you – are you prepared to have ~~dog-poo~~ put in your best shoes?

3. Hold on – could you have Maradona and Messi in the same team?

THE DECISION

Who is going to be the **attacking midfielder** in your squad?
Draw them here, giving the trophy to your first choice,
and the medal to your second choice.
Don't forget to add their names to the silverware!

MUSIC

Great teams thrive on a great atmosphere. It starts on the coach to games and continues on in the dressing-room before the match. And **nothing** builds an atmosphere like the right music.

You'll need something uplifting. Something that gets your superstars pumped. Nothing **too slow**, so they're all nodding off like babies. Nothing **so fast** that they get knackered busting flashy dance moves.

Build your playlist here. Perhaps include the tune that will play in the stadium as your team runs out. And **give the playlist a name** so everyone knows what magic is coming through the Bluetooth speaker.

1 ....

2 ....

3 ....

4 ....

5 ....

6 ....

7 ....

8 ....

CHANTS

A team is nothing without its supporters. Supporters are nothing without **a song**. Pick from the classics, tweak an old favourite or come up with your own. **Write the words out down below and pump up the volume.** Your team needs roaring on. As do you.

CLASSICS TO BORROW

................................Barmy army!

................................Barmy army!

Add your name here x2

A love song from the fans to you, telling you how much your hard work is appreciated. So definitely worth considering.

CLAP CLAP!
CLAP-CLAP CLAP!
CLAP-CLAP
CLAP-CLAP

Simple but effective. Works best with shorter club names, or one bit of them, e.g. City, Tottenham, Wednesday.

Add your team name here

And it's...

FC...

We're by **far** the greatest team the **world** has **ever** seen...

Usually when this is sung you know your team isn't really the greatest team the world has ever seen. You're just having fun, plus taunting your rivals. Except in your case, it actually **is** the greatest team the world has ever seen. It's fact. **Wallop.**

SHORT AND SWEET

Sometimes the greatest chants are the simplest. If it's easy to remember and can be bellowed by thousands of people in the stadium, it will work.

'He's one of our own. He's one of our own. Harry Kane, he's one of our own.'

'Mané!' (da da da-da dada) 'Mané Mané!'

'Sergio. Sergio! Sergio. Sergio!'

POP SONG TUNE, YOUR OWN WORDS

You may or may not have heard of **'Seven Nation Army'** by the White Stripes. But you **will** know the tune, because it works a treat with everything from star players' surnames to full club names. It's the one that goes, **'Da,** da da dada, **daah,** da …' **YouTube it.** It'll make sense.

Pick a tune you love, re-do the words to make it about your team, and make it a new classic.

My chant:

Such a great position, this one.

You're not after an out-and-out goal-scorer, although all these players can score mountains of goals, and one of them has scored more goals than anyone else in history.

You're not after a pure playmaker, someone who just makes chances for someone else, although they will lay on heaps.

You're not after a winger, although they'll be able to go wide when they need to, and it's not just a skilful dribbler, although they will be able to dribble skilfully.

You're after all of those, which is why the second striker is such a hard position to get right and such a beauty when you do. Goals made and scored. Strong in the air. All manner of cheeky tricks.

Some of the greatest players of all time have been second strikers.

Let's find out why.

CLUBS LEEDS UNITED, JUVENTUS, ROMA, CARDIFF CITY, HEREFORD UNITED

COUNTRY WALES

CAPS 38 **PEAK** 1955-1959

HONOURS 3 ITALIAN LEAGUE TITLES, 2 ITALIAN CUPS

JOHN CHARLES

Plenty of superstar strikers have **released records.** No one has released one **quite** like John Charles. It was called **'Sixteen Tons'**, and it's **moody.** But you're not picking him for his **singing**, useful though it might be in the dressing-room after big wins. You're picking him for the goals he scored and how much defences **feared** him.

Big. Strong. Fast, with **magic little bursts of acceleration**, brilliant off either foot. Far more skilful than **most** big players. **So** all-round talented that he could play in **defence** as well as up top, although he'd be **wasted** there.

And **so many goals** – 42 in 39 appearances in 1953–54 for Leeds. Then a **British record move** to Juventus at a time when almost **no** British stars played abroad.

Juventus fans voted him their **greatest ever foreign signing**, part of a front three in Turin they called the **Holy Trident.** They had a special nickname for him too – **'Il Gigante Buono'**, the Gentle Giant, because he was such a lovely man. A **totem** for any team.

GOAL SCORING	GOAL MAKING	STYLE	YOUR RATING
9/10	8/10	7/10	/10

CLUBS RIVER PLATE, HURACÁN, MILLONARIOS, REAL MADRID, ESPANYOL

COUNTRY ARGENTINA (LATER PLAYED FOR COLOMBIA AND SPAIN)

CAPS 41 (31 FOR SPAIN) **PEAK** 1953-1958

HONOURS 5 EUROPEAN CUPS, 8 SPANISH LEAGUE TITLES, SPANISH CUP, 2 ARGENTINE LEAGUE TITLES, 3 COLOMBIAN LEAGUE TITLES, SOUTH AMERICAN CHAMPIONSHIP

ALFREDO DI STÉFANO

This is straightforward. Di Stéfano would run your team for you. Taking the ball off your goalkeeper or full-backs. **Dictating** play. Finding pockets of **space** to play in and with all the turns and **tricks** to make the most of them. Absolutely loved a **back-heel**.

A ridiculous stat: Alfredo scored in **five** consecutive European Cup finals. In the last of these he scored a **hat-trick** as Real Madrid beat Eintracht Frankfurt 7–3 in what might be the greatest performance by a club side in history. Scored **216 league goals in 282 games** for Real, **twice** winner of the Ballon d'Or. Not bad for a short bald bloke.

And he was once **kidnapped** in Venezuela and played in a match **the day after** being released!

There could be **issues.** He very much liked to be the **main man**. If he thinks another player is getting **more attention** than him he won't be doing much passing. But then you might not **need** any others. Not when Di Stéfano is **this good.**

| GOAL SCORING | 9/10 | GOAL MAKING | 9/10 | STYLE | 8/10 | YOUR RATING | /10 |

CLUBS SANTOS, NEW YORK COSMOS
COUNTRY BRAZIL
CAPS 92
PEAK 1958-1965, 1968-1970
HONOURS
3 WORLD CUPS,
2 COPA LIBERTADORES,
6 BRAZILIAN LEAGUE TITLES

PELÉ

Oh, what a player! Oh, what a man! No single player is so **adored** across the world or **achieved** as much. Pelé made his debut for Brazil aged 16 and won his **first World Cup** with them at 17. He won his **last** with them aged 29. No one has won **more** World Cups or scored **more** goals for Brazil. No one has scored more goals **ever** than his **1,281,** and he didn't even take many **penalties**.

But you get **everything** with Pele. He can dribble, he can volley, he can **hang in the air** and head the ball with the **force** of a Conor McGregor punch.

No one wore Brazil's number 10 like him. No one scored goals like his **flick-and-volley** in the 1958 World Cup final or his **header** in the final 12 years later, or celebrated with the same **total joy**.

'I told myself before the game, he's made of **skin and bones** just like everyone else,' said the Italy defender who tried to mark him that day. 'But I was **wrong.'**

GOAL SCORING	10/10	GOAL MAKING	8/10	STYLE	10/10	YOUR RATING	/10

CLUBS AJAX, BARCELONA, LOS ANGELES AZTECS, WASHINGTON DIPLOMATS, LEVANTE, FEYENOORD

COUNTRY THE NETHERLANDS

CAPS 48 **PEAK** 1970-1976

HONOURS 3 EUROPEAN CUPS, 9 DUTCH LEAGUE TITLES, 6 DUTCH CUPS, SPANISH LEAGUE TITLE, SPANISH CUP

JOHAN CRUYFF

Right. Three European Cup wins, **three times** winner of the Ballon d'Or. The man who delivered **beautiful football** at Ajax and then **beautiful football** at Barcelona, with beautiful football for the Netherlands in between and **everywhere else.**

He **invented** one of the great pieces of skill. More than **40 years** on, the **Cruyff Turn** – body going one way, outside foot **flicking** the ball the other – still regularly beats defenders. He also realised that football is about where the ball **isn't** as much as where it **is.** He will find **space** for your team and he will use it **brilliantly**.

He'll get you goals, **special goals.** On the training ground he'll invent **drills** to help you, like the **rondo circle** and tiki-taka passing. He used to talk about players showing **insight**, trust and **daring**, and he'll bring **all that** too.

He won't **like** being told he's wrong. **Then again**, he hardly ever **was.**

| GOAL SCORING | 8/10 | GOAL MAKING | 9/10 | STYLE | 10/10 | YOUR RATING | /10 |

CLUBS CELTIC, LIVERPOOL
COUNTRY SCOTLAND
CAPS 102 **PEAK** 1977-1982
HONOURS 3 EUROPEAN CUPS,
6 ENGLISH LEAGUE TITLES, FA CUP, 4 LEAGUE CUPS,
4 SCOTTISH LEAGUE TITLES, 4 SCOTTISH CUPS,
SCOTTISH LEAGUE CUP

KENNY DALGLISH

You get strikers now who **don't celebrate** when they score. Or rather, they run off **without smiling**, or stand still, **staring** back at the fans. **Not Kenny Dalglish.** When he scored goals, the **pleasure** was all over his face – **massive** grin, both arms up, the **happiest** man in the world. When he scores goals for you, like he scored the winning goal in the 1978 European Cup final, like he scored a **record number of goals** for Scotland, you'll be **beaming** too.

There are **so many reasons** why he was voted by Liverpool fans as their **greatest ever player.** Perfect technique. A right foot that fired **thunderbolts**, a left boot that could bend and **place** the ball where it liked. **Strength** and determination. Never fast on the deck but with a brain that **raced** far ahead of others.

And oh so modest. 'It was a privilege to even go to Liverpool and play,' he once said. 'It was a **privilege** to win.' That's why they called him **King Kenny.** Bring him back to his **throne.**

| GOAL SCORING | 9/10 | GOAL MAKING | 9/10 | STYLE | 9/10 | YOUR RATING | /10 |

CLUBS WASHINGTON FREEDOM
COUNTRY USA
CAPS 276 **PEAK** 1995-2000
HONOURS 2 WORLD CUPS, 2 OLYMPIC GOLDS, 1 US LEAGUE TITLE

MIA HAMM

The strike-rate that saw Hamm notch **158 international goals** would come in **very handy** for a new team like yours. Maybe even **more** important would be her **144 assists,** a USA record. It's almost the **perfect definition** of a second striker: **makes** goals, **scores** goals. Pelé made his international debut at 16, Mia at **15.** He won his first World Cup aged 17. She won hers at **16.**

On the pitch she was elegant, athletic and **full of tricks**. Off it she was the most **marketable** female footballer of all time. She could help bring a **big-name sponsor** to your team. Her right foot was the **blasting** machine. She could bend them and angle them but she preferred to **smash** them. She was obsessed with **success**, and she will drive your team on in the same **relentless** way.

Oh – she linked up instinctively with Kristine Lilly and Joy Fawcett, among your options at left midfield and centre-back. That's one **world-beating triangle** to build a winning team around . . .

| GOAL SCORING | 8/10 | GOAL MAKING | 9/10 | STYLE | 9/10 | YOUR RATING | /10 |

CLUBS MALMÖ, AJAX, JUVENTUS, INTER MILAN, BARCELONA, A.C. MILAN, PARIS SAINT-GERMAIN, MANCHESTER UNITED, LA GALAXY

COUNTRY SWEDEN

CAPS 116 **PEAK** 2005-2011

HONOURS EUROPA LEAGUE, 4 ITALIAN LEAGUE TITLES, 4 FRENCH LEAGUE TITLES, 2 FRENCH CUPS, 2 DUTCH LEAGUE TITLES, DUTCH CUP, DUTCH LEAGUE CUP, SPANISH LEAGUE

ZLATAN IBRAHIMOVIĆ

Look, **no one** is disputing what Zlatan is going to bring on the pitch. If they are, show him his overhead kick for Sweden against England, or his **endless** dribble for Ajax against Breda in 2004. **The skills are insane.** The goals came **everywhere** – the only man to score for **six** different teams in the Champions League. His career has taken him to the greatest clubs in the world.

But. Massive but. He's had **multiple bans** for kicking, stamping and fighting, mainly because he **keeps** kicking, stamping and fighting. He's **arrogant,** even by his own admission, and he falls out with **rivals** and he falls out with **team-mates.** He loves José Mourinho but he absolutely **hates** Pep Guardiola. And **no one** hates Pep Guardiola.

He'll probably fall out with **you.** He certainly won't **stay** very long. But the time he **is** there he may work **miracles** that no one else could pull off. 'Only God can judge me' reads one of his many tattoos. **It's a big ask, but you may have to too.**

| GOAL SCORING | 9/10 | GOAL MAKING | 7/10 | STYLE | 9/10 | YOUR RATING | /10 |

CLUBS VASCO DA GAMA, SANTA CRUZ, UMEÅ IK, LOS ANGELES SOL, SANTOS, FC GOLD PRIDE, WESTERN NEW YORK FLASH, TYRESÖ FF, FC ROSENGÅRD, ORLANDO PRIDE

COUNTRY BRAZIL

CAPS 151+ **PEAK** 2006-2010

HONOURS

COPA LIBERTADORES, 7 SWEDISH LEAGUE TITLES, 2 US LEAGUE TITLES, 3 COPA AMÉRICAS, 2 UEFA WOMEN'S CUPS, SWEDISH CUP

MARTA

Imagine being the manager who has a **six-time World Player of the Year** on their team. Imagine being able to pick the **first player ever** to score at five World Cups, or the striker who has scored more goals at World Cups than **any other player** in history.

That's Marta. Tricks, **feints**, step-overs. That's Marta too. So is **creativity**, a magical left foot, an ability to play **anywhere** across the front line with a **ruthlessness** never seen before.

And she'll inspire your troops too. There's her **speech** at the 2019 World Cup, when she called on the **next generation** of female talent to push on and **fill the space** behind her. There's the goal against the USA in 2007, where she **spins**, flicks the ball over her shoulder, runs into space, throws in an **outrageous** dummy, swerves past a third defender and then **crashes** home the finish. It's like having Ronaldinho, Ronaldo and Pelé **all rolled into one.** Pelé made the Brazil number 10 jersey his own. Marta has somehow **enhanced it further.**

GOAL SCORING	GOAL MAKING	STYLE	YOUR RATING
10/10	8/10	8/10	/10

MANAGER'S NOTES

1. Pelé's real name was Edson Arantes do Nascimento. Can you learn it by heart, as <u>so many</u> football obsessives have?

2. Zlatan's your **tallest** option here. Although John Charles might be the best in the air. But does Pelé's leap <u>out-do them all</u>?

3. You don't 'have' to pick Kenny Dalglish. But if you don't, can you deal with the fact that no Liverpool fan will ever talk to you again?

THE DECISION

Who is going to be the **second striker** in your squad?
Draw them here, giving the trophy to your first choice,
and the medal to your second choice.
Don't forget to add their names to the silverware!

Being selfish is usually a bad thing. You get told off. People don't want to hang around with you. Be generous, they tell you. Share with others.

That's all true. Unless you're a finisher.

Finishers know it's a team game but they know too that they don't have to care. All finishers have to do is finish. Nothing else matters.

Nothing else matters because football, when it comes down to it, is about goals, and scoring more of them than the other team. If you've got a player in your team who takes almost every chance they get, who is always in the right place at the right time, who is as lethal as a poisonous snake, you will be deadly too.

And all goals count. True finishers can score big goals and small goals. They understand that a toe-poke from three inches counts the same as a thunderblast from 30 yards.

Just score. Lots. Like this lot.

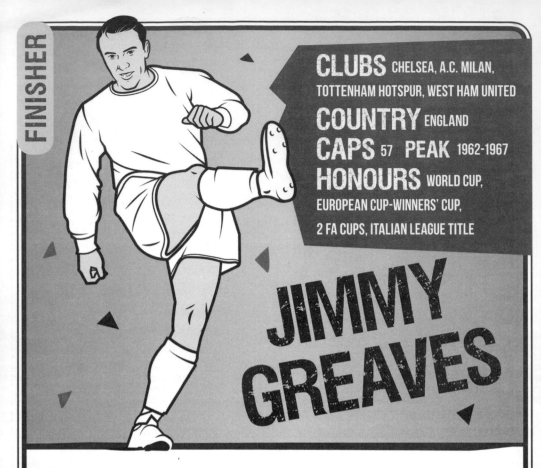

CLUBS CHELSEA, A.C. MILAN, TOTTENHAM HOTSPUR, WEST HAM UNITED

COUNTRY ENGLAND

CAPS 57 **PEAK** 1962-1967

HONOURS WORLD CUP, EUROPEAN CUP-WINNERS' CUP, 2 FA CUPS, ITALIAN LEAGUE TITLE

JIMMY GREAVES

Finishers have to be cool. They have to **keep their head** when all around are panicking, pick out the **unguarded** corner of the net and apply **exactly** the right touch when your brain is shouting **'GOAL!'** and **'QUICK!'** and **'HOOF IT!'**

There was **no cooler cat** in front of goal than Jimmy. It was almost as if there were **no** defenders or 'keeper in front of him and no **crowd** on its feet. He would **look up**, work out the angles and **casually** clip it home. Again. And **again.** And **again.**

The **most hat-tricks** for England, the most **goals** in top-flight English football, the most goals in history for Spurs. A goal on his **First Division debut**, a **hat-trick** in his first team debut, goals on his debut for Milan and West Ham. Such a **clean** striker of the ball, off the deck, on the volley, with his **head.**

Had it not been for **injury** in the group stages, **he** would have been the man who won the 1966 World Cup for England.

SHOOTING **10/10** HEADING **8/10** DEADLINESS **9/10** YOUR RATING 10

CLUBS BUDAPEST HONVÉD, REAL MADRID
COUNTRY HUNGARY
CAPS 85 **PEAK** 1958-1964
HONOURS OLYMPIC GOLD,
3 EUROPEAN CUPS, 5 SPANISH LEAGUE TITLES,
SPANISH CUP, 5 HUNGARIAN LEAGUE TITLES

FERENC PUSKÁS

You look at clips of Puskás and you can **wonder** if you've got the right man. **Short, a bit tubby round the middle.** Looks like your **grandad.**

Then the **stats** slap you round the chops: **84 goals in 85 international matches**, **514 goals in 529 league matches** in Hungary and Spain. Voted best player at the 1954 World Cup, the man who scored **four goals** in a European Cup final (with his mate Alfredo Di Stéfano getting the other three).

How will he **score** you those goals? Loads with his **hammer** of a left foot. **Plenty** with his head. A **bundle** with his little tricks and skills, which he perfected by practising with a **tennis ball.**

Warning: you might have to **comfort** opposition 'keepers after matches. When Puskás later **coached** a team in Canada, in his mid-50s, his shots were still **so hard** that it **scared** his players.

SHOOTING **10/10** HEADING **7/10** DEADLINESS **9/10** **YOUR RATING** /10

CLUBS AJAX, A.C. MILAN
COUNTRY THE NETHERLANDS
CAPS 58 **PEAK** 1987-1992
HONOURS
EUROPEAN CHAMPIONSHIP,
2 EUROPEAN CUPS, EUROPEAN CUP-WINNERS' CUP,
3 DUTCH LEAGUE TITLES, 3 DUTCH CUPS,
3 ITALIAN LEAGUE TITLES

MARCO VAN BASTEN

If you were a manager who had Marco in your team at his best **you were winning trophies. Fact.**

Some finishers are pure **fox-in-the-box**. All their goals come **inside** the six-yard box. That's fine, except Van Basten could score those and **also** ones on the run from the **edge** of the box, or with **outrageous volleys**, or with **overhead kicks** that made you want to shout, **'WHAT ARE YOU DOING, YOU BEAUTIFUL MADMAN?'**

He used to get **kicked. A lot.** It's why he **never played again after an injury at just 28.** So get someone in your team to **look after** him, to have a quiet word with any defender who wants to stop him with **sly kicks** and fouls because they can't stop him **any other way.**

And the **wondrous goals** will come for you. **Three times** winner of the Ballon d'Or, and he didn't even get to play at his physical peak. Brilliant off **either** foot. Absolute **team player.** Elegant. **How could you not?**

SHOOTING **10/10**   HEADING **910**   DEADLINESS **9/10**   YOUR RATING **/10**

CLUBS CRUZEIRO, PSV, BARCELONA, INTER MILAN, REAL MADRID, A.C. MILAN, CORINTHIANS

COUNTRY BRAZIL

CAPS 98 **PEAK** 1995-1999

HONOURS 2 WORLD CUPS, EUROPEAN CUP-WINNERS' CUP, UEFA CUP, SPANISH LEAGUE TITLE, SPANISH CUP, DUTCH CUP, 2 BRAZILIAN CUPS, 2 COPA AMÉRICAS

RONALDO

Say **'Ronaldo'** now and it's all **confusion**. You don't think about a Brazilian striker. You don't talk about a bloke whose weight **ballooned** after he retired from football.

So let's spell it out. The **original** Ronaldo, at his best, **redefined** what a finisher could do. No more hanging around the box. No more **waiting** for others to create the chances. Ronaldo would come **deep.** He'd pick up the ball on halfway. He'd set off at **interstellar** speed, **swerve** and smash through the opposition ranks and **not stop** until he was in the area and ready to **smack** it home. **Honestly.** You couldn't believe what you were watching, which is why they called him **The Phenomenon.**

World Player of the Year aged just 20. **King** of the **elastico** and **step-over.** Literally making defenders and goalkeepers **fall over** with his skills.

He did it all. Let him do it **all over again for you.**

SHOOTING	1010	HEADING	8/10	DEADLINESS	10/10	YOUR RATING	/10

CLUBS INDEPENDIENTE, ATLÉTICO MADRID, MANCHESTER CITY
COUNTRY ARGENTINA
CAPS 97+ **PEAK** 2011-2017
HONOURS OLYMPIC GOLD, EUROPA LEAGUE, 4 ENGLISH LEAGUE TITLES, FA CUP, 4 LEAGUE CUPS

SERGIO AGÜERO

It's funny – you watch Sergio, and he's **always there** when the ball comes into the box. He's never at the **back post** when it's at the front post, and he's never at the **front post** when the cross is landing in the middle. He's **exactly** where the pass ends, or the header falls, or the ball **bobbles**.

And it's **not** an accident. He's like a **scientist** of scoring. He's a **mathematician** of modern football. He's always in the right place because he's **figured it out**, seen the angles, **worked out** the gaps. **Shifting** the ball to make a little space, striking it as **cleanly** as any human ever has.

The result? A pure finisher to **transform** your team as he transformed City. The club's **record scorer**, a man who once scored **five times between the 42nd and 62nd minute** of a Premier League match, the man who scored the most important goal in City's history when he slotted that late, **late** winner against QPR in 2012. He's **best mates** with Messi. What a potential combo. The perfect end to a **perfect** team.

| SHOOTING | 9/10 | HEADING | 7/10 | DEADLINESS | 8/10 | YOUR RATING | /10 |

CLUBS MONACO, JUVENTUS, ARSENAL, BARCELONA, NEW YORK RED BULLS

COUNTRY FRANCE

CAPS 123 **PEAK** 2000-2005

HONOURS WORLD CUP, EUROPEAN CHAMPIONSHIP, CHAMPIONS LEAGUE, 2 ENGLISH LEAGUE TITLES, 2 FA CUPS, 2 SPANISH LEAGUE TITLES, SPANISH CUP, FRENCH LEAGUE TITLE

THIERRY HENRY

Speed. So **essential** to a top finisher, so **integral** to everything Henry will bring to your party. He started as a **winger**, so there's **dribbling** to go with the pace, and there's an ability to **cut in** off the right or – more often – the left, and then **bend** shots into the top corner, the goalkeeper always **stretching** but never quite getting there.

There's the invention of a player who wants to score from everywhere: the **flick-up** and volley against Man United, the **swerving** run from deep inside his own half against Spurs. There's the ability to **play on his own**, if you want your second striker to drop a little **deeper,** like Dennis Bergkamp used to.

There's the **numbers.** No one has ever scored more goals for Arsenal, no one has ever scored **more goals for France**. The king in the Gunners team that became known as the **Invincibles** for going through an **entire** Premier League season unbeaten. He'll bring **style** too. With his skills and finishing, with his **attitude** and accent. **Va-va voom!**

| SHOOTING 9/10 | HEADING 8/10 | DEADLINESS 8/10 | YOUR RATING /10 |

CLUBS TOTTENHAM HOTSPUR
COUNTRY ENGLAND
CAPS 45+   **PEAK** 2016-

HARRY KANE

Harry Kane **confused** people at the start of his career. He wasn't the **best** at any one thing. He wasn't about pace. He was never **flashy**.

And then the **goals** came and **kept** coming, and **suddenly** it became clear. He wasn't the best at any **one** thing, because he was **9/10 at everything.** He didn't **need** pace because his **brain** took him to the right place like lightning. He wasn't flashy because he just wanted to **work harder** to get even better.

Kane is the **all-round** **striker** that **every** team wants. He can play **on his own** up front, holding the ball up, laying it off. He can **run** at defences and **place shots** from outside the box. He can get his **head** on the end of crosses, and he can **bury them** from five yards out.

Best of all? He always finds the **corners**. There is no **luck** with Harry Kane. It's all practice and it's all **perfection**.

He might not be England's highest ever scorer yet. **But he will be** one day.

| SHOOTING | 9/10 | HEADING | 9/10 | DEADLINESS | 9/10 | YOUR RATING | /10 |

CLUBS KOLBOTN, STABÆK, TURBINE POTSDAM, LYON
COUNTRY NORWAY
CAPS 66 **PEAK** 2015-
HONOURS 4 CHAMPIONS LEAGUES, 5 FRENCH LEAGUE TITLES, 4 FRENCH CUPS, NORWEGIAN CUP

ADA HEGERBERG

It took Leo Messi 66 games to **score 50 goals** in European competition. It took Cristiano Ronaldo 91 games. **It took Ada Hegerberg 49.** The Brazilian Ronaldo **inspired** Thierry Henry. Thierry Henry **inspired** Hegerberg, and you can see the **talents** streaming through – coming from **deep** at pace, steps and **tricks** outside the box, a **ferocious** shot to finish it off.

Hegerberg was always **obsessed** with the little details. It's why she will **practise** so hard in your team and why she was the **first ever winner** of the Ballon d'Or Féminin. Tall and strong, **deadly** with her right foot, she is only getting started too. Marta is still scoring goals for Brazil at 33. **Hegerberg is nine years younger. Wow.**

She is a woman of **principle**. She has **refused to play** for Norway since 2017, even missing the 2019 World Cup, because she felt the country's football association was not treating women's football **seriously** enough. She'll **set the standards** for your team. And she will **keep** scoring goals. It's what she does.

SHOOTING **9/10**   HEADING **7/10**   DEADLINESS **9/10**   YOUR RATING **/10**

MANAGER'S NOTES

1. Do you need pace up top, or have you got plenty <u>elsewhere</u> in your team?

2. Do you want your finisher to take pens? Harry Kane barely misses them. Van Basten took 54 in his pro career and scored a crazy 51 of them.

3. Does your second striker prefer playing more on the right or the left? Do you want your finisher to be the other way round?

THE DECISION

Who is going to be the **finisher** in your squad?
Draw them here, giving the trophy to your first choice,
and the medal to your second choice.
Don't forget to add their names to the silverware!

PICKING YOUR CAPTAIN

Great teams need **great leaders**. And great leaders are almost always great players, which is why there are **so many** sensational captains among the options for your team.

You could probably choose **a whole team of captains**. But that would cause arguments when it came to deciding who should lift trophies, plus it would make the centre-circle rather **crowded** when the ref calls the skippers in for the pre-match coin toss. Also, since the captain is the one who leads the team out onto the pitch, and **11 legends** walking out side-by-side take up an awful lot of **space**, there's a high chance that they could get wedged in the tunnel.

Awkward.

So how should you choose who wears the armband for the greatest football team ever? Try a couple of these pointers for size:

Admin

It's not all waving gleaming trophies about. The skipper has more dull jobs than a classroom assistant. Handing out tickets for players' families. Organising the Christmas party. Collecting fines when players have been late. If they're not hard-working, if they're not good with numbers, they might not be the leader for you.

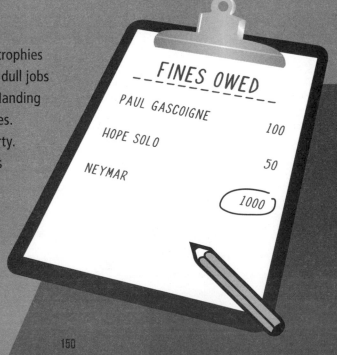

```
_____FINES OWED_____

PAUL GASCOIGNE
                           100
HOPE SOLO
                            50
NEYMAR
                        ( 1000 )
```

Bravery

You've got to lead from the front. If your captain pulls out of tackles or falls over without being touched, what sort of example is that to the rest of the gang? (Sorry, Neymar, this may be bad news for you.)

Big chat

Captains can inspire teams with amazing speeches in the dressing-room. They can drive them on with endless encouragement on the pitch. They can persuade a ref not to show red cards or to definitely give a penalty. A big mouth is not always a bad thing.

Respect

From the other 10 players, from the fans, from the manager. Does absolutely everyone look up to this character? That's a promising sign. Very, very promising.

Add your captain's name to the arm band

SUBSTITUTES

You're the boss. You know your football. This is where you get to choose your **super-subs** – three players not on the original lists who you want to bring to your greatest team ever.

* *

```
            SCOUTING REPORT:
            ---------------------------------
Who to start and who to bring on? Sometimes
the RIGHT SUB can be the difference between
a massive win and a heartbreaking loss. When
MANCHESTER UNITED came from behind to win the
Champions League in 1999, BOTH their goals came
from subs — Teddy Sheringham and Ole Gunnar
Solskjaer. And Germany's win over Argentina in
the 2014 World Cup final came courtesy of
ANOTHER late sub, Mario Göetze.
```

* *

NAME:

POSITION:

CLUBS:

COUNTRY:

REASON:

NAME:

POSITION:

CLUBS:

COUNTRY:

REASON:

Maybe it will be
a **forgotten hero** from the past.
Maybe it's a **genius young talent** you've spotted that you
reckon will go on to become one of the very best. Possibly it's just
a blatant bit of **bias** towards your favourite player in the team you
support. **It's your call, Gaffer.**

Fill in their stats, draw a picture and write down
the three reasons why they're in.

NAME:

POSITION:

CLUBS:

COUNTRY:

REASON:

ASSISTANT COACHES

There's a lot for you to be thinking about as manager of the greatest team the world has ever seen. Why not call up an **assistant coach** to give you a hand with selection, tactics and training?

Here are eight of the finest footballing brains to ever walk the planet. They can barely move for the trophies they've won. Choose the one that'll work best with your preferred style of football and general vibe, get them a tracksuit with their initials on the chest and **add their name to your very special list.**

HERBERT CHAPMAN

PEAK 1923-1933

BIG WINS 4 ENGLISH LEAGUE TITLES, 2 FA CUPS

Good old Herbert. The first modern football manager, a coach who'll get your players fit and keep them involved in tactics, he likes a counter-attacking style. Always stylish in full suit and waistcoat, he was also famed for an excellent scouting network to dig out new players and get the lowdown on the teams you'll be facing.

RINUS MICHELS

PEAK 1968-1974

Invented the beautiful way of playing the game known as Total Football. Can be strict with players, and not a bundle of laughs, but he'll want the football to look good and the players to truly showcase what they can do. Ideal if you're picking Marco van Basten, Johan Cruyff, Rudi Krol or Frank Rijkaard, as he brought the best out of all of them.

BIG WINS EUROPEAN CHAMPIONSHIP, EUROPEAN CUP

BRIAN CLOUGH

PEAK 1977-1981

Brian's not used to being a number two. He's used to being right, all the time. He'll also have a lot to say for himself, which is why his nickname was Old Big Head. Go with it, because as a manager he was a genius. Players loved him. He made ordinary ones into superstars and medium-sized clubs into giants. While telling everyone how good he was.

BIG WINS 2 EUROPEAN CUPS, 2 ENGLISH LEAGUE TITLES

ALEX FERGUSON

PEAK 1993-1999

BIG WINS 2 CHAMPIONS LEAGUES, 13 ENGLISH LEAGUE TITLES

Maybe the greatest British manager of all time. He'll be about great attacking football, about fast wingers and clinical strikers, and he'll move with the changing times – this is a man who won his final Premier League title 20 years after his first. He does also lose his temper, however, so either keep in his good books or let him be in charge of discipline with the players. Also useful to have around if you need a few extra minutes at the end of the match – there's a reason they call it 'Fergie time'…

ARRIGO SACCHI

PEAK 1987-1994

Loves a 4–4–2 formation, loves a team that defends high up the pitch and presses their opponents hard. He'll be magic focusing on your defence, but also keeping all your players working hard for each other. Can be stubborn, but usually when he knows he's on to something. Massive influence on Pep Guardiola and Jurgen Klopp; big success with Van Basten, Maldini, Baresi and Rijkaard.

BIG WINS 2 EUROPEAN CUPS, ITALIAN LEAGUE TITLE

JILL ELLIS
PEAK 2015-2019

The driving force behind the USA's dominance of women's football. Will bring all the experience of the first coach since the 1930s to win back-to-back World Cups, plus is used to handling big characters like Hope Solo and Megan Rapinoe. Likes attacking football, brilliant at getting the best out of players on the biggest occasions of all.

BIG WINS 2 WORLD CUPS

JÜRGEN KLOPP
PEAK 2017-

So much enthusiasm, so much love for his players and so much love back. Your team will feel special with Klopp on your side and he will be a constant bundle of energy and fun for you. Prefers a 4–3–3 formation and loves a high pressing style, borrowed from Sacchi, but done with even more speed and relentlessness. He calls it heavy-metal football. A no-brainer if you're picking Mo Salah, Virgil van Dijk or Andy Robertson.

BIG WINS CHAMPIONS LEAGUE, 2 GERMAN LEAGUE TITLES

PEP GUARDIOLA
PEAK 2009-

Charismatic, cool and all about football that makes your heart sing for joy, Pep would be a friend, wise counsellor and inspiration. Takes great players and gets them playing at a fresh level of wonder, whether it's Leo Messi, Raheem Sterling or Sergio Agüero. He'll want your goalkeeper to be as comfortable on the ball as a midfielder, and your midfielders to be able to play anywhere. Might not stick around forever, but while he's there, your job will be so much easier.

BIG WINS 2 CHAMPIONS LEAGUES, 3 SPANISH/3 GERMAN/2 ENGLISH LEAGUE TITLES

My Assistant Coach:

YOUR LOOK

All those assistant coach options have strong styles.

You think Pep and you think **smart** round-neck jumper over shirt, or that **funny chunky-knit** grey hooded cardigan-coat. You think Brian Clough and it's a **green sweatshirt**. Sir Alex? **Red and black Manchester United tie**. Rinus Michels was partial to a **navy blazer**, Jill Ellis a **long-sleeved** grey T-shirt. Klopp, a Liverpool **raincoat** with Liverpool cap and **Liverpool** tracksuit bottoms.

You? This is the beautiful thing. You can **borrow ideas** from those coaching legends or you can go **entirely your own way**. Draw your look here.

Now that is outstanding management.

You've chosen your **starting XI** and your subs, its formation, kit, mascot and badge. The **chants** are being chanted, the **playlist** being played. That newly designed stadium is **heaving**.

FINISHER

LEFT-MIDFIELDER WINGER

CENTRAL MIDFIELDER

LEFT-BACK

CENTRE-BACK STOPPER